DATE DUE

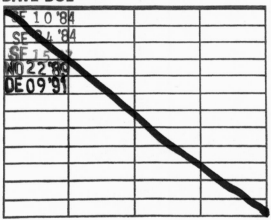

SE 10 '84		
SE 24 '84		
SE 15		
NO 22 '89		
DE 09 '91		

New Treasury
of
BASKETBALL DRILLS
from
TOP COACHES

Also by the Author

Attacking Zone Defenses in Basketball
Complete Handbook of Sports Scoring and Record Keeping

New Treasury
of
BASKETBALL DRILLS
from
TOP COACHES

Compiled and Edited by

Jack Richards

Parker Publishing Company, Inc.   West Nyack, N.Y.

Library of Congress Cataloging in Publication Data
Main entry under title:

New treasury of basketball drills from top
    coaches.

    1. Basketball coaching — Addresses, essays,
lectures. I. Richards, Jack W.
GV885.3.N47 796.32'3'077   82-2156
ISBN 0-13-615864-1 AACR2

Printed in the United States of America

WHAT THIS NEW TREASURY WILL DO FOR YOU

Some years ago I wrote *Treasury of Basketball Drills from Top Coaches* which presented the favorite practice drills of some of the country's leading basketball coaches. The response to that book was extremely gratifying. I have talked with a large number of coaches since that time and many of them have commented favorably on that book and asked for another. These coaches indicated that the book had served as a valuable aid in their daily coaching because it provided new ideas to supplement their own.

For this reason I have again contacted top coaches from all parts of the country and asked them to contribute their favorite drills to be included in a book for their fellow coaches. More than 100 successful and respected coaches from the high school, junior college and college levels have generously contributed their favorite basketball drills which I am proud to pass on to you.

Among those coaches who have contributed to the 42 offensive drills are Dean Smith, Denny Crum, Jack Hartman, Gene Bartow, Bill Foster, Ted Owens, George Raveling and Hank Raymonds.

Digger Phelps, Eddie Sutton, Lute Olson, Bud Presley, Rollie Massimino, Jerry Pimm, Marv Harshman and Dick Harter are just a few of the 28 coaches offering their favorite defensive drills. And, if this weren't an all-star coaching clinic already, the remaining Fast Break and Combination Drill sections include the favorites of Dick DiBiaso, C.M. Newton, Jim Dutcher, Stan Morrison, Lee Rose, Don Haskins, Jim Boeheim and Carroll Williams.

In addition to these college coaches, there are also drills from such legendary high school coaches as Lofton Greene of Michigan whose career record is 645-146, Bert Jenkins of Gulfport, Mississippi who is 579-102, Robert Hughes of Texas with a record of 532-101, and John Locke who has won more than 700 games as a Kansas high school coach.

This book will serve you as an invaluable coaching aid to which you will refer again and again.

Jack Richards

CONTENTS

PART II. DEFENSIVE DRILLS

10

CONTENTS

New Treasury
of
BASKETBALL DRILLS
from
TOP COACHES

Part I

OFFENSIVE DRILLS

JOHN WEINERT
Bowling Green State University

John Weinert began his coaching career in 1962 at Rufus King High School where, during four seasons, he compiled a 65-19 record and three regional championships. In 1966 he moved to Ripon College and recorded 76 wins against 55 losses in six years of coaching. After this he accepted the head job at St. Joseph's College where he remained for four seasons. His 72-39 record included three NCAA bids and "Coach of the Year" honors. He accepted his present position at Bowling Green in 1976, and he was named "Coach of the Year" in his conference his first season.

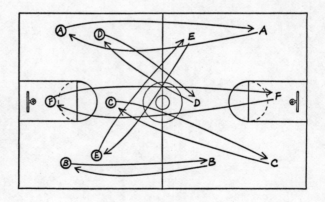

Diagram 1

BOUNCE AND JUMP DRILL: The team is divided into two groups. The players on the X side have a jump rope and the players on the Y side have a ball. A is paired with A, B with B, etc. On the whistle all X side players jump rope while the Y side players dribble low and under control. At the sound of the next whistle, the players sprint to the other side to exchange, jumpers becoming dribblers and dribblers becoming jumpers. On each whistle a change is made. The drill consists of two 2-minute periods of activity with a 1-minute rest in between.

Special Value of the Drill: The players work hard but have *fun* so the drill goes quickly. It's a good conditioner while emphasizing ball handling skills and eye, hand, and foot control.

DICK HUNSAKER
Weber State College

Dick Hunsaker is in his fifth year as an assistant basketball coach at Weber State College. A three-year letterman and team captain in his senior year at Weber State, Coach Hunsaker has played a major role in the 70-22 won-lost record, three Big Sky Conference Championships, and three appearances in the NCAA Tournament during his stint as assistant coach. When he served one season as head junior varsity coach, he guided the squad to their second best record in the school's history.

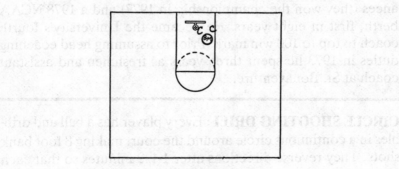

Diagram 2

BUMP DRILL: To run this drill you need two football hand-held blocking pads. Place the big man with a ball in the "power" area by the basket. Place coaches, managers, or extra big men on each side of him with their blocking pads. The drill is initiated with the big man being bumped with the blocking pads, and at the same time he must execute a power shot. Once he shoots, he must immediately rebound the ball regardless of whether he has missed or made the shot. He comes all the way down to gather his balance, then thrusts himself back up again, shooting another power shot. The bumping with pads is continuous, and the amount of force exerted with the bump is predicated on the ability of each big man. The drill is continuous for 30 seconds.

Special Value of the Drill: This drill is excellent in developing the ability of big man (or any player) to maintain balance while being bumped in the "power" area by the basket. Also, the big man must maintain his concentration on the basket and not allow the bumping to distract him.

JAMES SATALIN
Saint Bonaventure University

A former backcourt star with the Bonnies, Jim Satalin has posted a 126-68 record in seven seasons as head coach at St. Bonaventure. He has led the Bonnies to two NIT appearances (they won the championship in 1977) and a 1978 NCAA berth, first in eight years. He became the University's fourth coach to top to 100 win mark. Prior to assuming head coaching duties in 1973 he spent three years as freshmen and assistant coach at St. Bonaventure.

CIRCLE SHOOTING DRILL: Every player has a ball and dribbles in a continuous circle around the court making 8 foot bank shots. They reverse directions after 1-1/2 minutes so that each player shoots from each angle on the court. It is also an opportunity to practice full-court ballhandling dribbles with both hands.

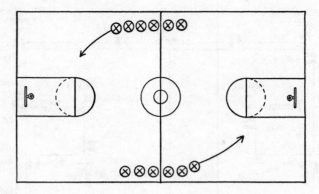

Diagram 3

Special Value of the Drill: This drill is essential for a fast break club who gets 10 foot bank shots at the end of a fast break. Each player will attempt approximately 35-40 shots in this drill. In the 2 to 3 minutes the drill is run, much is accomplished since it is continuous and everyone is involved.

BOB ZUFFELATO
Marshall University

Bob Zuffelato coached at Conrad High School in West Hartford, Connecticut, Woodland (Michigan) High School and at University High School in Ann Arbor, Michigan, before joining the college ranks as freshman coach at Hofstra University in New York. Two years later, he accepted a similar position at Central Connecticut State. After two seasons as an assistant at Boston College, he assumed the head coaching duties. During his six years at Boston College his teams twice appeared in the NCAA regionals and finished third in the NIT in 1974. Prior to assuming the top spot at Marshal, Zuffelato served as an associate head coach to Stu Aberdeen.

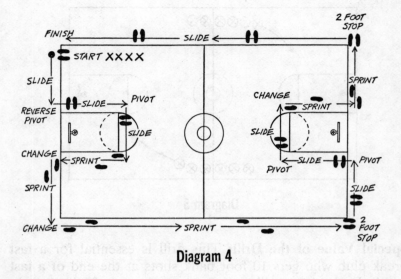

Diagram 4

SLIDE AND SPRINT DRILL: The players start in one corner of the court on the baseline. They assume a defensive stance, then slide to the lane and reverse pivot. They slide up the lane to the foul line and reverse pivot. They slide to the opposite side of the lane and change direction. Then they sprint down the lane to the baseline and change direction. They sprint to the sideline and change direction. They sprint to the sideline to the opposite baseline and come to a two-foot stop. They then slide to the lane and reverse pivot. Next they slide up the lane to the foul line and reverse pivot. They slide to the opposite side of the lane and change direction. Now they sprint to the baseline and change direction. After this they sprint to sideline and come to a two-foot stop. Finally, they slide the whole sideline, slapping the floor as they slide.

Special Value of the Drill: This is a great conditioning drill, a fine defensive drill, and in general a sound *fundamentals* drill emphasizing slides, change of direction, sprints, reverse pivots, and two-foot stops.

LOFTON GREENE
River Rouge High School, River Rouge, Michigan

Lofton Greene's basketball coaching career began at Center High School in Kentucky in 1940. In two years his teams were 16-14. From there he moved to New Buffalo High School in Michigan. In 1943 he became the head basketball coach at River Rouge High School. In a career that spans 37 years he has compiled an amazing 645 wins against only 146 losses. This includes 12 Michigan State Class "B" Championships and 5 State Runner Up positions. During this time he was named "Michigan High School Coach of the Year" in 1961 and in 1972. In 1972 he was honored by his fellow coaches as "National High School Coach of the Year."

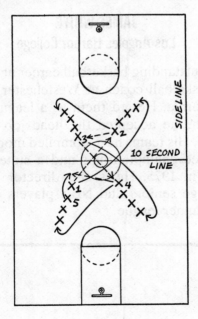

Diagram 5

DIAMOND PASSING DRILL: Using the one-hand, chest, or bounce passes, the drill is run as follows: X1 passes to X2 and breaks fast to the right to the rear of the line headed by X2. X2 passes to X3 and breaks fast to rear of that line. X3 passes to X4 and breaks fast to the left to the rear of that line. X4 passes to X5 and breaks left to the rear of that line. The drill continues as long as the coach likes. Each receiver is taught to break out to meet the ball. Corners can be backed up to teach any type of pass at any distance. Four balls may be used to teach dribbling with either hand. The players can dribble out of each corner and execute all types of pivots in center circle.

Special Value of the Drill: This drill teaches a great deal and requires very little time for organization. In this formation we can teach all types of passes, receiving, dribbling and pivoting.

JAMES WHITE
Los Angeles Harbor College

After an outstanding basketball career at USC, Jim White became the basketball coach at Westchester High School in Southern California. He led them to a league championship in 1965. In 1969 he accepted the head job at Los Angeles Harbor College. His teams have compiled more than 200 wins, three conference championships and a state Junior College Championship in 1975. He is also director at a Pro tryout camp for college seniors and NBA players qualifying for a Los Angeles summer league.

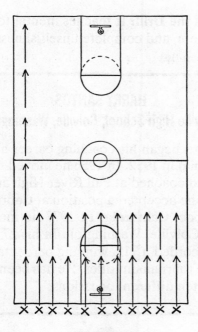

Diagram 6

DIVE AND SLIDE DRILL: *Teaching Players how to Dive on the Floor for the Ball:* Line the players up at the end of the court in a crouching position or squatting position with their finger tips touching the floor for balance. The technique is to lean forward, extend the arms and hands to pull oneself onto the floor, and slide on the stomach. *Keep the chin up!!* Use the sweat on the jersey to slide. In using the extended arms and hands the players pull with the palms of both hands, ending up with them at their side. The progression is a series of belly slides the length of the court. *Keep the chin up!!* For the future: Dive Sliding Contest from a run.

Special Value of the Drill: It teaches mental toughness, familiarity with the floor, and complete unselfishness for the team.

HARRY SANTOS
Colville High School, Colville, Washington

Harry Santos began his coaching career at Tulelake High School (California) in 1952. In 1956 he moved to the Fall River District (CA) and coached at Fall River High and Burney High until 1972 when he accepted a position at Cabrillo Senior High School in Lompoc, California. In 1977 he moved to Colville High School in Colville, Washington. In his 27 years as a head coach he has recorded a 71% winning percentage, nine league titles and twelve tournament titles. He has been named "Coach of the Year" on ten different occasions.

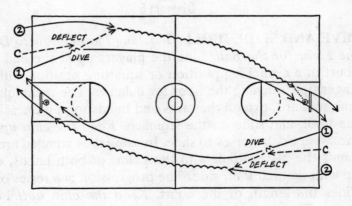

Diagram 7

DIVE DRILL: The Coach rolls the ball to about the head of the key at an angle as shown in the diagram. Player #1 (inside line) sprints, dives, and deflects the ball up ahead to teammate #2. 2 scoops up the ball on the dead run and dribbles hard to the basket for a lay-up. #1 gets up quickly and sprints after the shooter in order to tap in a possible missed shot. The players go to the ends of opposite lines at the other end of the floor. The drill is run on both sides of the floor at the same time.

Special Value of the Drill: The drill successfully teaches aggression in a loose ball situation. It helps make players unafraid to hit the floor and teaches them to get up quickly and continue to play.

LEN WILKINS
Hartnell College

Len Wilkins' coaching career began at Mission High School in San Luis Obispo, California. After one season he moved to Orland (California) High School in Orland where he spent four seasons. From there he moved to Montgomery High School in Santa Rosa, California, where he remained for six seasons. In 1968 he accepted the position as head basketball coach at Hartnell College in Salinas, California. His record includes 11 championships — 7 at the high school level and 4 at the college level.

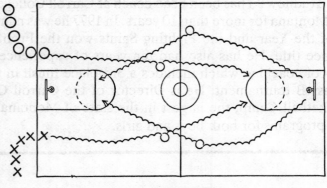

Diagram 8

DRIBBLE AND SHOOT DRILL:

1. Break the squad into two teams.
2. Each line will dribble to half court righthanded, cross the ball behind the back to a left handed dribble to the top of the key. The player must make a jump shot at the top of the key. If he misses, he rebounds and comes back to shoot until he makes the jumper. After making the shot, he must make a foul shot.
3. As soon as the player makes the foul shot, he returns to the other end repeating the same routine as previously described (right/left dribble, jumper and foul shot). He then passes the ball to the next man in line.
4. The first team to finish is the winner.

Special Value of the Drill: The drill provides an opportunity to work on jump shooting and foul shooting under pressure. You can put a high price on losing with laps or liners. It's still a fun drill and may best be used at the end of a long, hard workout.

JIM TRUDNOWSKI
Carroll College

Jim Trudnowski has been head coach at Carroll College in Helena, Montana for more than 10 years. In 1977 he was named Coach of the Year and the Fighting Saints won the Frontier Conference title. He has also had ten years of experience in high school coaching which includes a 3rd place finish in the state Class B tournament. He is Director of the Carroll College Basketball Camp, the largest in the state of Montana. It includes programs for both boys and girls.

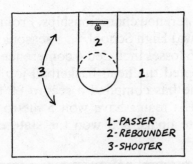

1- PASSER
2- REBOUNDER
3- SHOOTER

Diagram 9

50-SECOND SHOOTING DRILL: This is a timed shooting drill (for 50 seconds) with two balls and three players to a basket. There is a shooter, a rebounder, and a passer at each basket. (1) *Passer* passes across court with the *overhead pass*. He wants to pass to the "shooting pocket" of the shooter. He counts field goals and field goal attempts for the shooter. (2) *Rebounder* rebounds each shot and passes to #1. (3) *Shooter* shoots at different distances (coach decides this and varies it). After each shot he moves a step. He always stays on the same side.

At the end of the 50 second period the coach calls "rotate" and the shooter becomes the rebounder, the rebounder becomes the passer, and the passer is now the shooter. We usually shoot the jump shot without the dribble, but we can add one dribble. It takes about three minutes to finish one side. Daily results are posted along with weekly and season totals.

_____

JOHN CARLE
Lincoln High School, Des Moines, Iowa

John Carle began his coaching career at Cosgrove (Iowa) High School in 1961. In two seasons his teams were 32-7 and had won two conference championships. From there he moved to Knoxville (Iowa) High School. In 8 seasons there his record of 96 wins and 65 losses included 4 conference championships. In 1971 he accepted the head basketball job at Lincoln High School, where he has compiled a record of 138 wins against only 37 losses. His teams have won 5 metro championships, been to two state finals, and won the state championship in 1975.

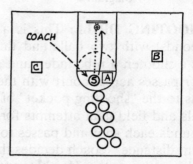

Diagram 10

50-SHOT DRILL: Only the top ten can shoot. Two balls are used. The coach passes a ball to the first man who is between the free throw line and the top of the key. He cannot dribble. He must immediately shoot a jump shot. He then rebounds his own shot while the coach passes the second ball to the next man who has stepped in. This player shoots and follows his shot. After that, the shooters who have rebounded pass to the next man in line. Each player will shoot five times. If two of his shots are left or right of the rim he must drop out of the top ten. The squad must make twenty-five of the fifty shots. Later the squad must make thirty, then thirty-five and so on as the season progresses. They shoot first from Area A, then B, and then C. Missed shots cannot hit the floor.

Special Value of the Drill: The drill is simple but has great value. It teaches quick shooting with emphasis on direction. It teaches the players to follow their shots. It teaches them not to put the ball on the floor before shooting. And above all, it teaches that scoring is a team effort. Each player must make over three of five if the team is to make its goal.

MIKE KUNSTADT
Irving High School, Irving, Texas

Mike Kunstadt began his coaching career in 1964 at Mona-hans (Texas) High, where his teams were 54-6. He then became an assistant at the University of Texas at Arlington. After one season he accepted the position as head coach at Carroll High School in Corpus Christi, Texas and compiled a record of 180 wins against 60 losses. He moved to Irving High School where his teams are 91-33, giving him a career record of 331-114. Among his many achievements and honors: winner of 12 tournament championships; twice selected as "Coach of the Year"; selected by the U.S. Jaycee's as "Outstanding Young Man of America"; and Director of the Texas Association of Basketball Coaches.

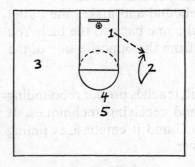

Diagram 11A

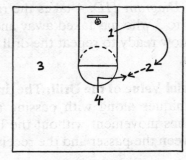

Diagram 11B

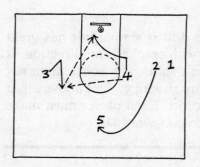 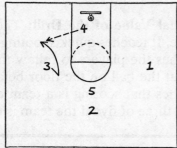

Diagram 11C   Diagram 11D

5-MAN REBOUNDING DRILL:

Diagram 11A: 1 starts the drill by putting the ball on the board and coming down strong, making a quarter-turn to the outside to hit 2 on the outlet pass. Insist that the players observe all the fundamentals of rebounding, passing, and receiving. 2 should fake away and come back to receive the pass from 1.

Diagram 11B: 4 fakes away and comes back to receive the pass from 2. After 1 makes the outlet pass he replaces the position previously occupied by 2.

Diagram 11C: 3 fakes away and comes back to receive the pass from 4. After 4 passes to 3, he fakes and then cuts down the lane looking for the return pass from 3. Upon receiving the return pass, 4 puts the ball on the board and rebounds. After 2 makes a pass to 4, he gets in the line behind 5.

Diagram 11D: 4 takes the rebound and makes the outlet pass to 3 who has faked away and come back to the ball. You are now ready to repeat the drill from the opposite side of the floor.

Special Value of the Drill: The drill teaches proper rebounding techniques along with passing and receiving techniques. It teaches movement without the ball and it emphasizes timing between the passer and the receiver.

DON KING
Washington High School, Cedar Rapids, Iowa

In 28 years of coaching, Don King has compiled 367 wins against 243 losses. At Washington High School he has won four conference championships and has had 12 consecutive first division finishes. His team won the State Championship in 1969, and had a 3rd place finish in 1978. He holds the Iowa AAA record of 40 consecutive wins in 1969 and 1970. On four occasions he has been named "Coach of the Year" in the Mississippi Valley Conference, and in 1969 he was named the High School Basketball "Coach of the Year" in District 2 by the National High School Athletic Coaches Association.

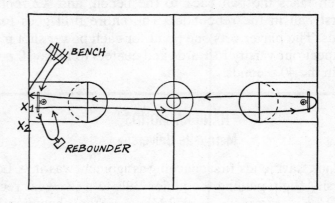

Diagram 12

40-SECOND DRILL: This is a very demanding drill. We like to use it twice a week before our first game is played and once a week thereafter, keeping results, making it competitive and measuring improvement. The McCall's Rebounder is set half-way between the baseline and free throw line extended on one side of the free throw line. On the other side is set an ordinary wooden bench. Players work in pairs with one performing and the other counting and assisting with the second basketball in the drill. The drill begins with X1 sprinting from baseline-to-baseline on the coach's starting command and the starting of the stopwatch. He has to make this run in 10 seconds or less to continue. On completing the trip, he picks the first basketball from the baseline and runs to the bench. He goes over the bench four times with the ball held over his head, explodes to the basket with no dribble, and power shoots it in. If he misses, he continues following until he scores. X2 has placed the second basketball on the McCall's Rebounder. X1 goes to the Rebounder and rips the ball off, fully depressing the arm, and again explodes to the basket, scoring on the power shot. He then takes the ball back to the bench, and X2 replaces the first ball in the rebounder. The entire drill goes for 40 seconds. The player gets one point for each power shot made. We expect our varsity forwards and centers to make 10 power shots in the 40 seconds.

HANK RAYMONDS
Marquette University

Hank Raymonds' first coaching assignment was at St. Louis University High, guiding the junior Bills to a five-year record of 108-23. His team won the 1952 Missouri State championship. Moving into the collegiate ranks at Christian Brothers College in Memphis, he turned the Bucs into a small college power with a six-year record of 111-47 and three NAIA district championships. He came to Marquette in 1962 as an assistant and served the Warriors as assistant coach until 1977. From 1964-73 he guided the Warrior jayvees to a remarkable 127-18 record. In his first season as head coach, Marquette was 22-7 and a participant in post-season NCAA play.

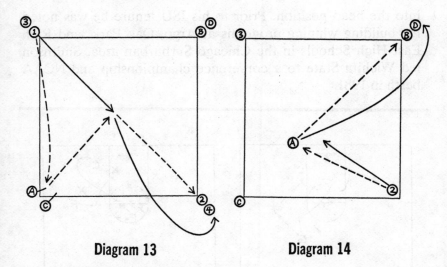

Diagram 13   Diagram 14

4-CORNER PASSING DRILL: 1 passes to A, cuts on a diagonal, receiving a pass from A at midpoint, then passes to 2 and goes to the end of that line.

A, after passing to 1, cuts on a diagonal, receives a pass from 2, then passes to B and goes to the end of that line. The player passes, receives a pass, makes a pass and then goes to the end of the line where he last passed.

A, B, C and D always stay in the same line as to 1, 2, 3 and 4. The player runs across in a straight line. He should wait for the ball in his corner to come to him. We build up to 3 balls and do the drill from 5 to 10 minutes each day.

GENE SMITHSON
Wichita State University

Gene Smithson became head basketball coach at Wichita State in 1978 after a three year stay at Illinois State University in Normal, Illinois. While there he posted a three year record of 66-18 and helped the Redbirds to two consecutive NIT appearances and a ranking of 13th nationally in 1977. He was an assistant at Illinois State for four years before moving into the head position. Prior to his ISU tenure he was noted for building winning programs at Argo, Oak Park, and Rich East High Schools in the Chicago Surburban area. Smithson led Wichita State to a conference championship and NCAA berth in 1981.

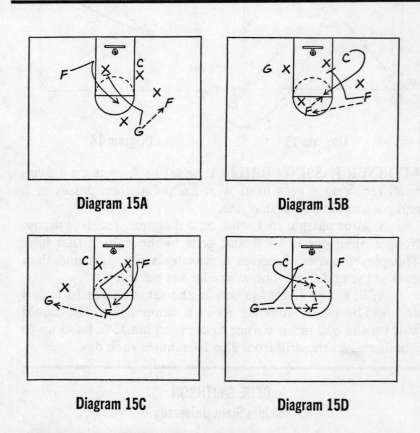

Diagram 15A   Diagram 15B

Diagram 15C   Diagram 15D

4-ON-4 CURL DRILL FOR CENTER: If you want to keep the center on post the majority of the time, he must curl back inside much of the time off picks by teammates. The guard hits the forward and executes a diagonal screen to bring the forward high (Diagram 15A). The forward then passes to the forward high in the lane and jam picks on the center's man. The center sets up his man and curls into the middle, looking for a pass from the forward (Diagram 15B). If the center doesn't get the ball and the defense switches, he sets up low on the opposite low post (Diagram 15C). If there is a mismatch on the pivot, the ball should go inside as quickly as possible. The forwards now interchange on the weakside. The guard reverses the ball to the forward and jam picks for the center who again curls inside (Diagram 15D). The drill can be run continuously, giving the center and other big men excellent work on their curl move.

LEON SPENCER
Henderson County Junior College

Leon Spencer has held his present position of Athletic Director and Head Basketball Coach at Henderson County Junior College in Athens, Texas for the past seventeen years where his teams have been consistently ranked in the nation's top twenty. His teams have won the Texas Eastern Conference Championship on seven occasions. He has twice been the Texas Eastern Conference Coach of the Year, in addition to being Region XIV NJCAA Coach of the Year in 1973. He coached in both the Texas Junior College All Star Game and the NJCAA All Star Game in 1977.

8-8-18 CONDITIONING DRILL:
Phase I (Time allocation 8 minutes)
   Run 8 horses (1 minute each). The player goes from the end line to the free throw line and back, 1/2 court and back, 3/4 court and back, to opposite end line and back

to far free throw line and back to far end line, etc., until
the player has worked his way back to the starting point.
This constitutes one horse.
REST **3** MINUTES
Phase II (Time allocation **6** minutes)
8 fartleks. Run one lap and jog one = one fartlek.
REST **3** MINUTES
Phase III (Time allocation **6** minutes)
18 laps around gym floor (one mile).

In each phase the player must complete it on time or
repeat the incompleted segment. This penalty reduces his rest
period. If a player becomes so far behind that rest periods
are absorbed, the workout is voided and must be done over
entirely at a designated time. This is a 26 minute workout.

LYNN ARCHIBALD
Idaho State University

Lynn Archibald coached basketball at Sierra Vista High
School in Baldwin Park, California and at Los Angeles High
School in Garden Grove. In 1971 he joined Jerry Tarkanian at
Long Beach State as a graduate assistant. The next year he
moved to Cal Poly San Luis Obispo as an assistant. In 1973
he rejoined Tarkanian at Nevada Las Vegas, where he was an
assistant for three seasons. In 1977 he was named head basketball coach at Idaho State University.

HOP COURSE: The player starts at the line and jumps to the
left box with two feet; he then proceeds to the right box, then
to the middle box, then to the left box. He continues in this
pattern until the course is completed. He can also do this while
hopping on one foot at a time. Other variations are shown in
diagram 16.

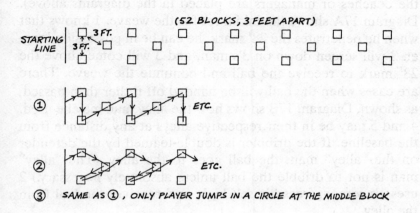

Diagram 16

Special Value of the Drill: This drill builds concentration, coordination, and stamina. It is a good warm-up drill for conditioning. The drill can be done in progression of two feet, left foot, and right foot on each hop course.

HERB LIVSEY
University of California at Irvine

Herb Livsey's background includes 12 years of high school coaching in Florida, Nevada, and California; 8 years of college coaching, with the majority of that as Head Basketball Coach at Orange Coast College in Costa Mesa, California from 1969 to 1976. He is currently the Assistant Basketball Coach at the University of California at Irvine. For 20 years he has been the Director and Owner of the Snow Valley Basketball School.

ICE DRILL: When I yell to put the ball "on ice," the players know to go to the 3-man weave, with the two other players taking "alley" positions (these positions are the same as where the coaches or managers are placed in the diagrams above). Diagram 17A shows the initial set for the weave. 1 knows that when he penetrates the 28' mark, he can be in possession longer. 2 will screen down on 3's man, and 3 will come above the 28' mark to receive the ball and continue the weave. There are cases when the ball will be handed off rather than passed, as shown. Diagram 17B shows how the alley man may be used. 4 and 5 may be in their respective alleys at any distance from the baseline. If the dribbler is double-teamed by the defender on the "alley" man, the ball goes to the alley. (The "alley" man is not to dribble the ball unless absolutely necessary.) 2 uses 1's screen, frees himself high, and receives the ball from the alley.

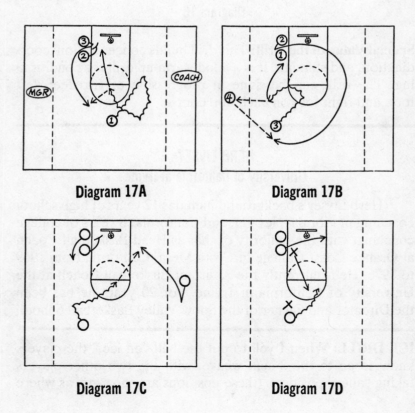

Diagram 17A   **Diagram 17B**

Diagram 17C   **Diagram 17D**

Note: When we drill ballhandlers, coaches and/or managers serve as "alley" men. Players not involved as ballhandlers or in defensing the weave are at the other end involved in other work.

Diagram 17C shows a scoring opportunity other than a dribble drive by 1, 2, or 3. Because most of my players have been right-handed, I have opened the right side for them in this position. If the double team comes from the right side, or there is extreme pressure there, that "alley" man may back door. This is a possibility, not something we definitely want to get. I would prefer the "alley" men to stay in their alleys. Diagram 17D shows the double team coming from the stack. When the two off-ball dribblers see this situation, they split. The dribbler may hit the open man. If the defensive men recover, the three ball-handlers go to a tight weave so as to screen for the jump shot, or they get back to their original set-up and continue to control the ball.

Important: The drill itself is execution of the dribbling, passing, and moving. I personally oversee this drill. I may have the offense keep the ball and direct the defense to foul, or I may have the offense try to score. If a foul is called, the player goes to the line to shoot 1 and 1; if a player scores, he goes to the line to shoot 1 and 1. If both are made, his team keeps the ball. Otherwise the ball is live. 21 points (2 points for a field goal, 1 for a foul shot). If the shot for the 21st point is missed, that team goes to zero and the game continues.

Special Value of the Drill: In the day of the 4-corner delay or stall pattern, I have stayed with a 3-man weave/free lance pattern to go against man-to-man pressure being used by an opponent who is behind. I prefer such a combination because I can control who will have the ball and what will be done with the ball. I determine early in the season what players are my best ball handlers and best foul shooters, and these are then the players who will have the ball in their hands when we control tempo and the clock at the end of the game. Our players know we will win it at the foul line. The drill requires fundamentals and handling pressure. Another reason I prefer this set-up is that I can place two more foul shooters in the "alley" positions; in addition to being an outlet for a pass, each is in position to face one of the referees in order to call a quick time out if need be.

LENNY FANT
Northeast Louisiana University

Coach Lenny Fant has been the basketball coach at Northeast Louisiana University for the past 22 seasons. Prior to that he coached one year at Louisiana College and three years at East Texas Baptist. His overall mark as a college coach is 388 wins against 258 losses. He is President of the Louisiana Association of Basketball Coaches, and was elected "Mr. Louisiana Basketball" by the Louisiana University Coaches. In the 1978-79 season his team was 23-6, winners of the Pacemaker Classic, winners of the 1st TransAmerica Conference Tournament, and participated in the NIT. Coach Fant finished his 18th straight winning season and was named "Coach of the Year" in the TransAmerica Conference and in District 8 by the coaches from the National Association of Basketball Coaches.

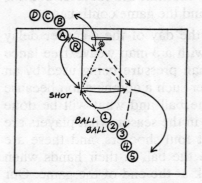

Diagram 18

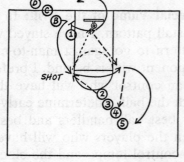

Diagram 19

INSIDE-OUT JUMP SHOT DRILL: Two balls are used to speed up the drill. A is the first shooter. After a jab step to set up the screen, he moves out to receive the pass from 1 for a jump shot. R is the first screener — he also rebounds A's shot and passes back to A. A passes the ball to 3 and goes to the end of the outside line. After 1's pass, he becomes a screener for B who is the next shooter. While the ball is being rebounded and passed out to the shooter, the next ball is being passed and shot.

Special Value of the Drill: I designed the drill because so much of our offense had options (after outside screens) with the shooter going away from the basket. The shooter should make the pivot and catch the ball already squared to the basket for the shot.

ELBERT RICHMOND
Mackenzie High School, Detroit, Michigan

Elbert Richmond has coached basketball at Detroit Mackenzie High School since 1972. His teams have compiled a record of 124 wins against 36 losses for a .775 winning percentage. Included in this record are six divisional league championships, four state district titles, three state regional championships, and the 1978-79 Class A State Championship.

JUMP SHOT SHOOTING DRILL: Four players are situated on each court in this Jump Shot Shooting Drill. Both baskets are used. The remainder of the squad lines up off the court awaiting the next game. Each of the players in the game has a ball. The object of the game is to make 15 jump shots before the other three players in the foursome. Each player must call aloud his score and retrieve his own shot. The game starts on the coach's whistle. When a player in the foursome hits 15 shots, the game is over. The winner stays on the court and the waiting players take their turn making up the shooting foursome.

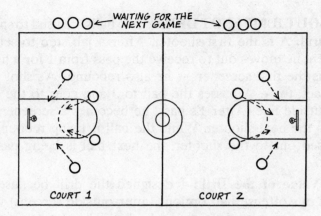

Diagram 20

Special Value of the Drill: The competitiveness of this drill develops better concentration and seriousness in shooting. It's also excellent for making shooters follow their shots.

JOE CIPRIANO
University of Nebraska

Joe Cipriano came to Nebraska in 1963 from Idaho where his teams posted a rebuilding trail much like Nebraska's: 10-16, 13-13 and 20-6. His 17-year record at Nebraska was 240 wins and 170 losses. While playing at Washington, he led the Huskies to three straight Pacific Coast division titles. After a short term at high school coaching, he returned to Washington as freshman coach for three seasons before coming to Idaho as the head coach in 1960. He served on the coaching staff in the Olympic tryouts in 1972 and in the Pan-Am Games in 1979. He was named "Coach of the Year" in the Big 8 in 1965 and 1978.

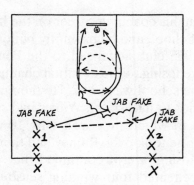

Diagram 21

ONE BOUNCE PICKUP: Two lines are formed outside facing the basket. The man with the ball (X1) jab fakes, dribbles the ball once, picks it up, and makes a pass to the man coming to meet the ball. The man without the ball (X2) jab fakes and then comes to meet the pass. After the pass, X1 will pick for X2. X2 stops after he catches the ball and jab fakes away from the pick by X1. X2 dribbles around the pick set by X1. X1 pivots toward the ball and then X2 and X1 pass the ball back and forth on the way to the basket for a layup.

Special Value of the Drill: This simple drill teaches several things: (1) It teaches the player to jab fake with and without the ball. (2) It teaches players to keep the foot down on a fake. (3) It teaches the players how to screen on the ball and how to pivot on the pick and roll. (4) It gives the players practice in passing and ballhandling.

RON RAINEY
University of Delaware

Ron Rainey played three years of varsity basketball and baseball at Penn State University where he was the Nittany Lions' leading scorer in 1957.

Rainey began his coaching career on the high school level at Chester High School, and he promptly built them into a title contender. His 1965 club advanced to the Pennsylvania State Semi-finals before losing to the eventual champions. His three-year record at the school was 52-17. He then moved to Wilkes (Pa.) College. Prior to his arrival, Wilkes had suffered through four futile years in which they won only 10 while losing 71. Three years after he took over, Rainey had them winning more than they were losing, and it continued that way as they enjoyed an unprecedented four winning seasons with Rainey's mark during that time period 52-38. In 1971, he became head basketball coach at Delaware University.

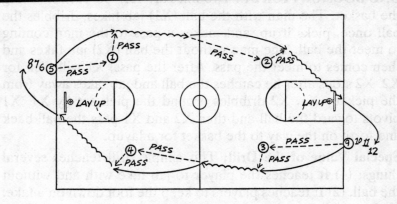

Diagram 22

PASS, DRIBBLE, AND LAYUP DRILL: A team must make 75 lay-ups in a two minute period. Using a full court area with every player involved, players 1, 2, 3 and 4 are stationed at the foul line extended. Players 5, 6, 7 and 8 are at the base-line on the left. Players 9, 10, 11 and 12 are baseline or the right. Two balls are required. Players 5 and 9 start the drill. Player 5 throws a pass to 1, gets a return pass, passes the ball to 2, gets a return pass and makes a lay-up. He then proceeds to the end of the line. This continues until 75 baskets are made in less than two minutes.

Special Value of the Drill: The drill is a good one to use at the end of practice because of the running and concentration needed to make 75 baskets. It gives four skills in one drill and the players can have some fun with their hustle and chatter.

DAN FITZGERALD
Gonzaga University

Dan Fitzgerald began his coaching career at Daniel Murphy High School in Los Angeles. He coached there four seasons before moving to San Jose's Archbishop Mitty High to assume the role of head basketball coach and athletic director. In seven seasons his high school teams compiled a record of 121-54. He was named "Coach of the Year" on two different occasions. In 1970 he moved to Santa Clara and directed the Bronco frosh to a 20-5 season. He then served as the head assistant at Gonzaga University for two years before returning to California and private business. In 1976 he again returned to Santa Clara as head assistant, helping the Broncos to return to the front as a major college power. In 1978 he was named the head coach at Gonzaga University.

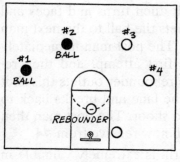

Diagram 23A

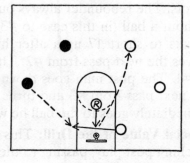

Diagram 23B

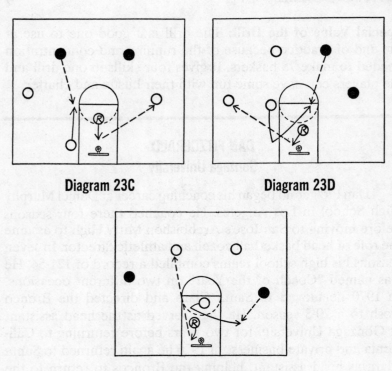

Diagram 23C   Diagram 23D

Diagram 23E

POST ACTION DRILL: In this drill there are two guards, two forwards, a post man and a rebounder. The weakside forward and the weakside guard have a ball. The post man comes ball side to receive a pass from #1. He then turns and faces and shoots. The rebounder always outlets the ball to the next man without a ball (in this case to #3). The post man immediately breaks to short 17 area after his first attempt and then receives the next pass from #2. The rebounder outlets this shot to #4. The post man goes down the lane and breaks back to the next pass from #3 and turns to shoot. The post man then immediately goes to the ball he will now receive from #4.

Special Value of the Drill: This drill is extremely valuable in teaching post play, passing to the post, and outletting the ball. It makes a player react quickly to the pass and quickly turn and face the basket.

GEORGE RAVELING
Washington State University

George Raveling was the captain of the 1960 Villanova basketball team and gained All-American honors. He played in the East-West All Star game before being drafted by the then Philadelphia Warriors. He served as an assistant coach at Villanova and the University of Maryland before becoming the head basketball coach at Washington State University. He is a member of the Black Hall of Fame. He was voted Pac-8 Coach of the Year in 1975, voted UPI West Coast Coach of the Year in 1975, and voted National College Coach of the Year in 1977 by the National Black Sports Foundation. He was honored by Villanova with its Distinguished Alumnus and Humanitarian awards. He has written two best selling books, *War on the Boards* and *A Rebounder's Workshop*.

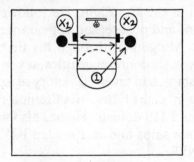

Diagram 24

POWER MOVE DRILL: Place a basketball beside the upper part of each foul lane box. Station a player or manager by each ball. A player (1) is positioned at the foul line. On the command of the coach, he will race and pick up one of the basketballs. As he picks up the ball, he will bring his two feet together and power up toward the basket. We require that this move be strong and aggressive. Once (1) shoots the first ball, he races across the lane to the second ball and performs the same movement. In the meantime, X1 rebounds the shot and places the ball back in its original position. X1 and X2 will always rebound the ball and place it back into position. We recommend each player do the drill for 30 seconds. This drill can be advanced from the power move to shooting hook shots and jump shots. We would move the ball to a slightly higher position along the lane for the hook or jump shots.

TED OWENS
University of Kansas

Ted Owens was a three-year letterman for Bruce Drake at Oklahoma from 1949 to 1951. He first came to Kansas at the start of the 1960-61 season as an assistant, and he was named head coach in 1964. He immediately made an impact guiding a very young Kansas team to an overall 17-9 record and second place finish in the Big Eight. He followed that with four 20-victory seasons and post-season appearances along with two Big Eight titles. Altogether, through his first 14 seasons, the Jayhawks have won six conference titles, seven Holiday Tournament Championships, had seven 20-victory seasons and advanced to post-season play eight times. His lifetime record at Kansas is 265 victories and 119 defeats. He has also won two Midwest Regional championships and in 1968 led KU to the runnerup position in the NIT.

PRE-GAME PASSING DRILL:

#1 has the ball and will start movement on pass to #4.

#4 will go high and pass or flip off to #5.

#5 will then go high and flip off to #2 who will come down to #4 area.

#2 will go high and flip off to #3.

#3 will go high and flip off to #1.

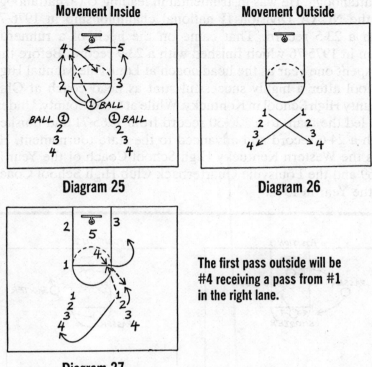

Movement Inside

Diagram 25

Movement Outside

Diagram 26

Diagram 27

The first pass outside will be #4 receiving a pass from #1 in the right lane.

Players continue ball handling under the basket and after each flip off by the high man, then that player comes toward outside line, receives the pass, passes right back to the next player and then spins to the outside and goes right back to flip position under, then to opposite side. The inside players will always stay inside and the outside players outside until the coach changes them. Thirty to forty-five seconds is a good time to change groups.

RALPH UNDERHILL
Wright State University

Ralph Underhill is in his third year at the helm of Wright State after spending six years as an assistant at Tennessee-

Chattanooga. He was instrumental in leading UT-Chattanooga to the NCAA Division II national championship in 1976-77 with a 23-5 record. That came on the heels of a runnerup team in 1975-76 which finished with a 23-9 record. Before this he spent one year as the head coach at Louisville Manual High School after a highly successful stint as head coach at Ohio County High School in Kentucky. While at Ohio County, Underhill led the team to a 126-30 record from 1965-71 and finished with a 24-6 record and advanced to the state tournament. He was the Western Kentucky High School Coach of the Year in 1969 and the Louisville Quarterback Club High School Coach of the Year in 1972.

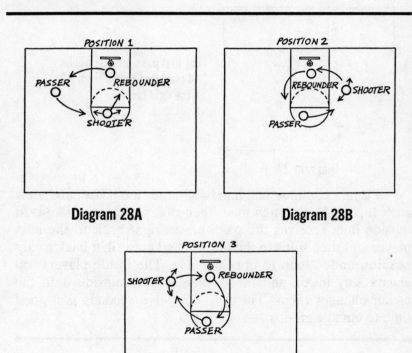

Diagram 28A   Diagram 28B

Diagram 28C

QUICK SHOT DRILL: There are three people at a basket and two basketballs are used. The three positions are shooter, passer, and rebounder. Each player has 55 seconds to shoot from each of the three spots (right, left, and the free throw line). The players have five seconds to rotate to a new position after the time period is up. The shooter goes to the rebounding position. The rebounder becomes the passer and the passer becomes the shooter. After all three shoot from the position, they change to another spot and continue the routine. The rebounder will count the number of baskets made while the passer records the number of shots attempted. The manager should record the percentage of each shooter. Each player should get off around 22-25 shots every 55 seconds. Do not allow the players to dribble. They should catch and shoot in one motion.

Special Value of the Drill: The players learn to get the 15' jump shot quickly. They also learn to shoot and get ready for another pass. It requires good hand and eye coordination in addition to good footwork. It keeps three people busy passing, rebounding and shooting while stressing teamwork among the group.

DON KING
Washington High School, Cedar Rapids, Iowa

Don King's 367-243 career record includes coaching stints at Hayfield, Iowa; Lisbon, Iowa; Robbindale, Minnesota; Nevada, Iowa; Coe College; and Cedar Rapids Washington High School. He has had four state tournament teams, including two 3rd place finishes and one State Championship. He is the recipient of 9 Coach of the Year awards! At Washington High School his record currently stands at 202-95.

"READ THE DEFENSE" DRILL: Our "Read the Defense" drill is normally a 5 on 4 drill with the 4 players on defense playing a box or 1-1-2 zone. We sometimes run it 5 on 3 or 5 on 6 also. We run two patterns that are common to us in both our zone and man-to-man offensive attacks. One is called "Rotation" which is shown with the wing-corner pass triggering the action (Diagram 29A). The other is very similar and is called "Reverse" and is triggered by the wing returning the ball directly to the point man and cutting through rather than going first to the corner.

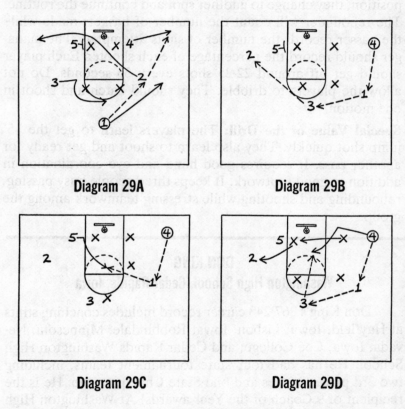

Diagram 29A   **Diagram 29B**

Diagram 29C   **Diagram 29D**

From there we try to reverse the ball as quickly as possible and READ THE DEFENSE and HIT THE OPEN MAN (Diagram 29B). We tell the 4 people on defense to vary their tactics from extreme sag into the middle to popping out into passing lanes to prevent reversal of the ball. Likewise, we instruct the back corner defender to vary his tactics on the baseline screen shown on the diagrams from setting behind the screen to fighting over it high or low and on occasion anticipating it and breaking over it early to pick up #2 as he receives the ball (or earlier). As a result of these varied attacks, the offense has to react accordingly. When perimeter passing lanes are contested effectively, this becomes the instant signal for the post man diagonally away from this action to "flash" into the middle (Diagrams 29C and 29D). We require a minimum of 4 passes before an outside shot can be taken, and we work hard to get it inside or to take an open 15 footer after such exploration. We normally run this drill at both ends of the playing floor and sometimes precede the above part of the drill with speed passing work with a weighted ball.

Special Value of the Drill: We particularly like this drill because it emphasizes many of the points we feel are essential to good offense:

1. Good crisp passing.

2. Reversing the ball from one side of the floor to the other.

3. Effective use of eye fakes and fake passes.

4. Post men reading the perimeter defense and flashing into the middle.

5. High-low options.

6. Passing the ball before taking the outside shot — working to get the high percentage shot.

7. Hitting the offensive board.

GENE BARTOW
University of Alabama in Birmingham

During six seasons of coaching in Missouri High Schools, Gene Bartow compiled an impressive 145-39 record, including a State Championship in 1957. He next spent three years at

Central Missouri State where his teams won 47 games while losing 21. In 1964 he moved to Valparaiso University and recorded 92 wins against 69 losses during six seasons. Following this, he became the coach at Memphis State. In four seasons his teams won 82 games while losing only 32. His 1973 team reached the "final four" in the NCAA Tournament and he was named national "Coach of the Year." After one season at the University of Illinois, he accepted the job at U.C.L.A. where, in two seasons, his teams were 52-9. His 1976 team again reached the NCAA final four. In 1977 he became head coach at the University of Alabama in Birmingham, which he led to an NCAA berth in 1981 with a 23-9 record.

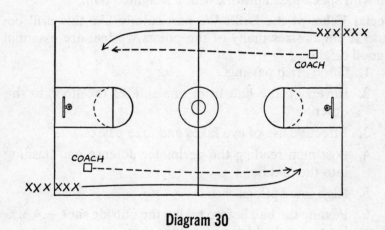

Diagram 30

RECOVERY AND LAYUP DRILL: The coach throws long passes ahead of the player streaking down the floor. The player has to run the ball down, *get ball control, get control of his body,* and *then* take the ball to the basket for a lay-up.

Special Value of the Drill: The drill teaches the importance of gaining *ball control* and *body control* before going for the lay-up.

BILL FOSTER
University of South Carolina

Following four seasons as a Pennsylvania high school coach, Bill Foster became head coach at Bloomsburg State, where he posted an impressive 45-11 record. Bill then developed winning programs at both Rutgers and Utah, reaching the NIT finals at the latter. As head coach at Duke University, Bill Foster reached the NCAA tournament 3 straight years, including a runner-up spot for the National Championship for which he was honored as national "Coach of the Year." A past president of the National Association of Basketball Coaches, Bill Foster is presently head coach at the University of South Carolina.

SCREEN DRILLS:

Using a Screen/or Setting a Screen: More and more teams employ pressure-type defenses in which the main objective is to force the offensive team out of the things they want to do. When this occurs, it means that players are forced into freelance situations. In this, players are generally forced into different forms of movement. At this time, players moving without the ball, in particular, should become aware of:

    a. using a screen to free himself.

    b. setting a screen to free a teammate (ready to roll back *toward* the ball as the man who sets the screen is usually open).

    c. vision of the defensive man playing him (backdoor is watching the ball, etc.)

Three types of screen that can be utilized are:

    a. *Lateral set screen* (Diagram 31): On this type of screen away, the screener should be ready to pop back toward the ball. If a switch occurs, hit and roll to the basket or the ball.

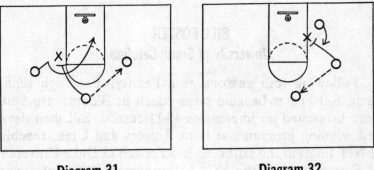

Diagram 31   **Diagram 32**

b. *Baseline jam and buttonhook low* (Diagram 32): Screen down along the baseline; if you are setting the screen, as you close in and "headhunt" the defensive man playing your teammate, stop and let your teammate use your screen so you don't get called for movement while setting the solid screen.

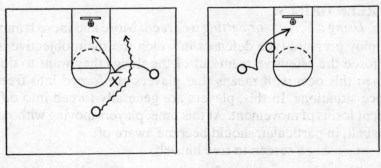

Diagram 33   **Diagram 34**

c. *The rear screen* (Diagram 33): Set from the rear (either facing the basket or facing the man you are setting the screen for); remember, the rules state you must give the defensive man one full step if you are out of the defensive man on the ball's vision.

Using Screens: always be ready to either set a screen to free a teammate or use one to free yourself.

a. *Change of direction* (Diagram 34): Fake one way to go the other direction more effectively; always keep your defensive man active and vision on you (takes away his "helping" power).

b. *"California" type screen* (Diagram 35): Screen away from ball using low or medium post position (passer — remember screener always open; be ready to roll opposite direction of the cutter back *toward* the ball).

c. *"Shuffle" type cut* (Diagram 36): Screener at the high post away from the ball; lead your man to him; change direction and speed to the hole.

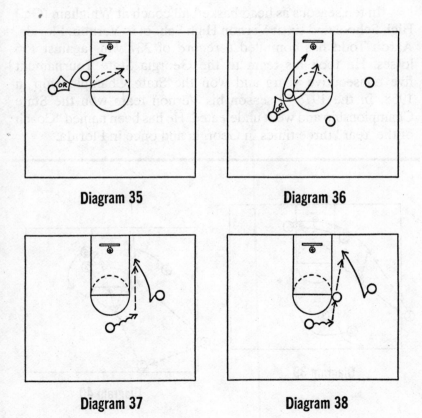

Diagram 35   Diagram 36

Diagram 37   Diagram 38

    d. *"Backdoor" type cut* (Diagrams 36 and 37):

       (off the dribble)

       (off the pass)

Setting a screen and using a screen needs constant attention through drill. Set up these situations and allow time for the players to work on the moves described.

AARON TODD
Vernon High School, Vernon, Florida

In ten seasons as head basketball coach at Whigham (Ga.) High School and six at Vernon High School in Vernon, Florida, Aaron Todd has compiled a record of 237 wins against 156 losses. He took his team to the Georgia State Tournament five consecutive years and won the State Championship in 1968. In the 1978-79 season his Vernon team won the State Championship and went undefeated. He has been named "Coach of the Year" three times in Georgia and once in Florida.

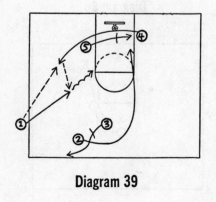

Diagram 39

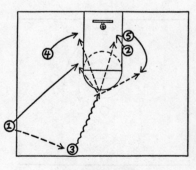

Diagram 40

SIDE COURT OUT-OF-BOUNDS PLAY:

1. 1st option: Look to hit #2 with a high lob pass at the block. Usually this is not open.

2. 2nd option (and best): #1 hits #4 on the wing and immediately breaks for the basket looking for a return pass from #4. #1 can usually get penetration for a ten foot jumper or create a 3 on 2 inside. #4 rebounds the left side; #5 rebounds the right side; #1 and #2 rebound the front.

3. 3rd option: If the above are not open, #1 hits #3 (watch the mid-court line) and looks for a return pass. If the return pass cannot be made, #3 starts penetrating dribble looking to hit #1 on his left or #5 on his right coming off a down screen by #2.

Special Value of the Drill: It is quick hitting (can score in 3 seconds). It has several options and works equally well against both man and zone defenses. The play takes no special personnel and all types of players can fit into a position.

DENNY CRUM
University of Louisville

In recognition of leading Louisville to the 1980 NCAA Championship, Denny Crum was named National "Coach of the Year" by Basketball Weekly. In Crum's ten seasons at Louisville, he had led them to the NCAA playoffs eight times, making it to the final four on three of those occasions. Louisville has won at least 20 games in each of Crum's ten seasons and his winning percentage ranks among the highest of all active college coaches. Prior to arriving at Louisville as head coach, Crum served five years as an assistant to John Wooden at UCLA.

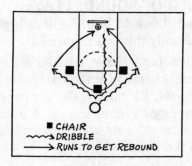

Diagram 41

SPEED SHOOTING DRILL: Place three chairs on the court as shown in the diagram. The player starts behind the middle chair. He dribbles with his outside hand from the middle chair to a side chair, squares to the basket, and shoots the jump shot. After shooting the ball he rebounds the shot and dribbles out around the middle chair with the opposite hand and goes to the other side chair where he executes a jump shot. The player continues to move from one side to the other. The drill lasts for one minute and the scores are kept and posted.

Special Value of the Drill: The purpose of the drill is to teach dribbling, shooting in balance and speed. It also builds conditioning and dribbling with both hands as well as the proper technique in shooting the jump shot.

JACK HARTMAN
Kansas State University

In seven seasons at Coffeyville Junior College, Jack Hartman recorded 150 wins against 46 losses. His National Championship 1961-62 team was undefeated at 32-0. In 1962 he moved to Southern Illinois where, in eight seasons, he compiled a record of 144-64. His 1966-67 team won the NIT. Championship. In 1970 he accepted the position as head coach at Kansas

State University. During his tenure he has recorded 169 wins against 84 losses. On three occasions (1971-72, 1972-73, and 1976-77) his team won the Big 8 Championship.

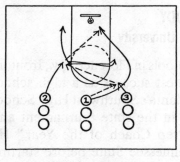

Diagram 42

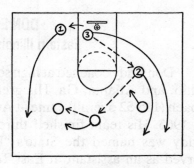

Diagram 43

3-LINE, HALF COURT LAYUP DRILL: There are three lines starting at half court with the wide men cheating down one stride for timing purposes. The middle man (1) starts the drill by passing to 3 and then following behind three. 2 moves in to meet the pass from 3. 3 makes a pass to 2 and follows behind for rebound position. 1 gets in position to receive a pass from 2. 2 makes a pass to 1 for a layup. 2 continues to free throw line extended to receive outlet pass from 3. 1 continues wide and starts a return to the end of the line. 3 makes overhead outlet pass to 2 and follows his pass. 1 goes to the end of the line. 3 is wide and continues to the end of the line. 2 passes the ball to the next middle man and stays wide to return to the end of the line. Middle man starts ball in opposite direction from which he received it for continuation of the drill. When players become familiar with responsibilities, use two balls.

Special Value of the Drill: This drill requires good ball handling, accurate passing, and quick thinking under pressure. It can be used as a good conditioning drill, also. The players must really concentrate when fatigued to maintain the quality of the drill. The coach must emphasize accurate, crisp passing in this drill to maintain timing. No dribbling! Ball need never touch the floor.

DON EDDY
Eastern Illinois University

Don Eddy coached at high schools in Florence, Ky., Ironton, Ohio, and Atlanta, Ga. His greatest success as a high school coach (115-52 overall) came at Atlanta's Southwest High School in 1965. His team finished third in the state tournament and Eddy was named the State's "Prep Coach of the Year." He served as an assistant at East Tennessee State before starting the rebuilding job at Eastern Illinois in 1969. He has directed seven Panther teams into post-season tournaments in his tenure at the NCAA II basketball power. 1979 marked the fifth straight year the Panthers competed in the NCAA II tourney, equalling the previous best national finish. Eddy's over-all collegiate coaching record, all at EIU, is 187-122, the second best winning percentage among nine previous Eastern cage coaches.

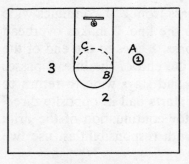

Diagram 44A

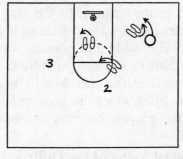

Diagram 44B

3-MAN REBOUNDING DRILL: Diagram 44A shows proper alignment of offensive and defensive players. 1 has the ball to start (coach or manager may shoot the ball also). 1 shoots the ball. Diagram 44B shows the alignment and proper movement of defensive players. A steps to make contact with 1 and pursues the ball. B pivots on the foot away from the ball and pursues ball to offside (seeing offside position filled, he will pick up middle rebound position and play bounce). C pivots on the foot away from the ball and picks up the offside rebound position.

LARRY HUNTER
Wittenberg University

A two year letterman at Ohio State, Larry Hunter was a member of OSU's 1969 NIT team. He served as assistant basketball coach at Marietta College before coming to Wittenberg in 1973. His three-year record as jayvee coach at Wittenberg was 34-4. In 1976 he was named head coach and his first squad won the NCAA Division III National Championship. For this achievement he was named "Coach of the Year." His four year record at Wittenberg is 91-21 and includes three Ohio Athletic Conference Championships. In 1980 he was named District Coach of the Year and Ohio Athletic Conference Coach of the Year. In his four years, Wittenberg has won either the regular season or conference tournament championship each season.

3-MAN REBOUNDING DRILL: When the ball is shot (should be from at least 15′) D must screen out O and rebound the shot. O works on offensive rebounding postion. Should he get the rebound, he plays 1 on 1 against D. Once D gets the rebound he becomes the next shooter by dribbling out to the wing for a shot. O now becomes the next "D" player, screening out S who has become the next offensive rebounder. The drill continues until the coach terminates it. It is best to use a rebounding bubble to keep the ball alive.

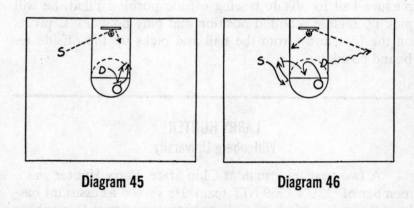

Diagram 45   Diagram 46

DON DONOHER
University of Dayton

Don Donoher came to the University of Dayton in 1963 as an assistant and was awarded the head position in 1964. After 16 seasons at the helm he has had only one losing season. His current record is 272-147 and it includes six seasons in which Dayton teams have won 20 games or more. Even more impressive is the Flyers' post-season tournament record under Donoher. Dayton has participated in eleven tournaments in Donoher's 16 years, with six NCAA and five NIT tournament berths to his credit.

3-ON-3 CONTINUITY: The ball begins with the coach. He passes to 03 and 01 makes a cut off 02's screen, either baseline or over the top. 02 holds the screen and then drifts out

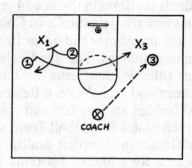

Diagram 47

to replace 01. 03 looks for 01 inside or goes one-on-one with his man, X3. If 03 does neither, he passes back to the coach, who reverses the ball to 02. Now 03 comes off 01's screen and the continuity is now on.

Special Value of the Drill: (Offense) Each player experiences a turn at the post as a screener or shooter, as an outside man with the ball either passing or going one-on-one, and as a cutter without the ball. (Defense) It gives the players work at defending an outside man with the ball and without the ball, a weakside man going off a screen, and an inside man flashing to the post. The defensive men can or cannot switch, depending on the coach's rules for the drill. Rebounding is also a big part of this drill.

DEAN SMITH
University of North Carolina

Dean Smith, national coach of the year in two of the past four seasons, has one of the greatest reputations in the history of the college game. In 19 seasons at Carolina, he has an amazing record of 415 victories against only 135 losses. That's a percentage of .752, the seventh best mark in history of any coach with over 300 victories. Under Smith, Carolina has reached the NCAA semi-finals six times in the last 14 years. In the same period Carolina has won the Atlantic Coast Conference regular-season championship nine times and never finished lower than second in the league standings. The Tar Heels have won eight ACC Tournament titles in that same stretch and have also captured five Eastern and one Western Regional crowns. Perhaps Smith's most famous accomplishment came in 1976 when he guided the United States Basketball Team to a sweep of the Summer Olympic Games in Montreal. Smith's Olympic victory was just another in a long line of his remarkable successes. His record in the last 14 years is 349-88. Carolina went to a national post-season tournament all 14 of those seasons. The Tar Heels won the NIT in 1971.

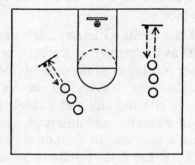

Diagram 48

TOSS-BACK SHOOTING DRILL: In this shooting drill we use toss backs or have someone throw the ball back. Each player has a ball. He passes it, gets it back, squares up and shoots. He then rebounds his own shot and goes to the end of the next line. You can position the toss backs at any place on the court.

JAMES VALVANO
North Carolina State University

After serving as an assistant basketball coach at Rutgers University and the University of Connecticut, Jim Valvano accepted the head job at Johns Hopkins University. He remained there for a year and then became the head coach at Bucknell University for three seasons. In 1975 he moved to Iona and began a rebuilding program. In four seasons he has compiled a 65-42 record. Coach Valvano has successfully rebuilt three programs and made them winners. At John Hopkins he gave them their first winning season in 25 years. At Bucknell and Iona he gave them their first winning season in ten years. At Iona they enjoyed their winningest season ever (23 wins) and made their first appearance in the NCAA regionals. Jim is now the head coach at North Carolina State in the tough ACC.

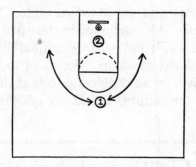

Diagram 49

25-SHOT DRILL: Player 1 moves from side to side. Player 2 is the rebounder and the passer. Player 1 will take 25 shots following this formula:

10 — no dribble jump shots
5 — one dribble jump shots
5 — more than one dribble jump shots
5 — anything goes (e.g., 2 dribbles to the right, spin dribble left and then a jump shot)/

Player 1 must move constantly and as if he were in a game. He must make 13 of 25.

Special Value of the Drill: The drill incorporates straight-up shooting, shooting off the dribble, shooting off individual moves. The constant movement helps conditioning, forcing a player to shoot when tired. The drill is challenging because the players must make over 50%.

RICH GRAWER
University of Missouri

From 1969 through 1979, Rich Grawer recorded 220 wins against 72 losses at De Smet Jesuit High School in St. Louis, Missouri. His teams won the Missouri State Championship in 1973, 1978 and 1979. Also included in this span is a third place finish in the State (1977) and two quarterfinal finishes (1971 and 1974). He was named Missouri "Coach of the Year" on two occasions. Rich is now an assistant coach at the University of Missouri and is the author of *Secrets of Winning Post Play Basketball.*

2-BALL OUTLET DRILL: A drill that involves two men in a game situation is the *Two Ball Outlet Drill.* One of the shooters (1), shoots the ball, trying to score. X screens out 0. If the ball goes in, X (the defensive rebounder) grabs the ball from the net before it hits the floor and fires it full court to 5 who shoots the uncontested layup. If the initial shot is missed, X outlets to the proper outlet guard (3 or 4 — depending on which side the ball caroms). The offensive rebounder (0) naturally adds a lot of pressure and resistance to X as he tries to do his job. After the defensive rebounder has outletted the ball, the opposite shooter fires the ball towards the basket. 1 and 2 continue to alternate shots as soon as the defensive rebounder has released his pass.

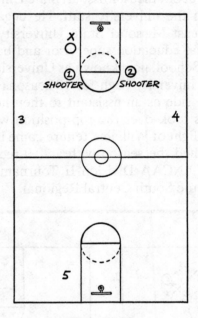

Diagram 50

It is advisable to begin running this drill without an offensive rebounder. Later the offensive man can be added. X should be kept in a rebounding position for as long as two to three minutes. This really becomes tough, especially if the shooters are hot. It is possible for the rebounder to have to throw 15-20 full court passes in a minute. Fatigue sets in. The coach should emphasize the arms-up technique when a rebounder is tiring. Keep the rebounder in the drill until he does it perfectly: arms always up, constant effort, good anticipation where the rebound will carom, good rebounding form, good outlet (not allowing the ball to hit the floor).

CARROLL WILLIAMS
Southeast Missouri State University

Carroll Williams has completed his fifth season as head basketball coach at Southeast Missouri State University. It marks his 29th year on the university staff. He began his teaching career at Southeast Missouri State University in the fall of 1960 as a physical education supervisor and basketball coach at College High School, now known as University High School. He coached at University High for 10 seasons before moving to the collegiate side as an assistant to then head coach Bob Cradic. Williams took over the top position when Cradic resigned. The highlight of Williams' tenure came in 1978-79 when the Indians finished the season with a 20-9 record and won a berth in the 1979 NCAA Division II Tournament. The Tribe finished third in the South Central Regional.

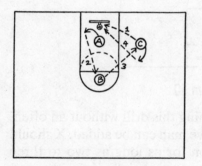

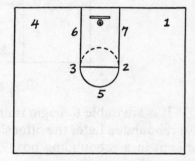

| Diagram 51A | Diagram 51B |

2-BALL SHOOTING DRILL: C is the shooter. B is the passer. A is the rebounder. C shoots from the various spots shown on Diagram 51B. He shoots, lands, moves, and receives the pass to shot again. He is always moving, turning to face the goal, getting his elbows in and his body behind the ball, etc. A

rebounds the ball and gets it to B. As soon as C shoots, B feeds the second ball to him for the next shot. The three men use two balls and keep them moving a lot. We shoot for 50 seconds, rotate, and change shooter.

Special Value of the Drill: It teaches concentration. It cuts down on the horseplay because the players must really keep their mind on what they are doing. It provides better and more intense effort in developing a shooting touch.

ROBERT HUGHES
Dunbar High School, Fort Worth, Texas

After graduating from Tulsa University, Robert Hughes became the head basketball coach at Terrell High School in Ft. Worth, Texas. His teams won 360 games while losing only 65. This included 9 district championships, a county championship, and three state championships. He was named "Coach of the Year" nine times in the district, one time in the county, and one time for the state. Coach Hughes then moved to Dunbar High School in Ft. Worth. During 6 seasons there he has compiled a record of 172-36. His teams at Dunbar have won 4 district championships, 2 regional championships, and have twice been runners up for the State Championship.

2-LINE PASS AND SHOOT DRILL: Two lines of players take a position at the sidelines near the mid-court line. The receiver (1) gets the pass at mid-court and drives for a shot. The trailer (2) from the same line rebounds the missed shot or takes it out of the basket if the shot is good and passes out to a new receiver from the opposite line breaking across mid-court.

The receiver should break across the middle only after the trailer has possession of the ball. The receiver can shoot a layup, jump shot, or pass back to the trailer who can then take a shot.

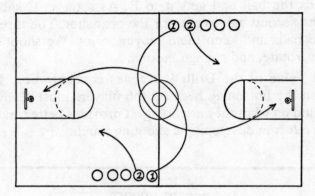

Diagram 52

Special Value of the Drill: So many things can be done from this all-purpose drill. We can shoot jump shots, layups, and set picks; make long and short passes; rebound the ball; and work on our player's speed.

SONNY SMITH
Auburn University

Sonny Smith began his high school coaching career in the hotbeds of prep basketball in North Carolina, Virginia, Indiana, and Kentucky. He put together a record of 126-87 over eleven years. In 1970 he moved to the West Coast and Pepperdine University as an assistant coach. There he recruited a group that came in to beat the freshman squads of UCLA, USC, Long Beach State and Nevada-Las Vegas. In 1971 he moved to Virginia Tech, where he remained as an assistant for five years and recruited most of the players for teams that won the National Invitational Tournament and made an appearance in the

NCAA tournament. His first head coaching job in the college ranks was at East Tennessee State University. In two seasons he took a team that had lost 20 games the year before he arrived to an 18-9 record and a share of the Ohio Valley Conference championship. He was named OVC Coach of the Year in 1978. Coach Smith is now the head coach at Auburn in the basketball-rich SEC.

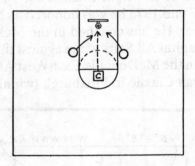

Diagram 53

2-MAN CUT THROAT DRILL: Two players line up facing the basket. The coach throws the ball up on the board and the players try to tip the ball in the basket (they are teammates on the first toss). As the ball goes through the basket, the player who retrieves it is now on offense while the other becomes the defensive player. The drill continues as the players rebound their makes or misses. The object is to see who has the most baskets at the end of one minute.

Special Value of the Drill: The drill is good for tipping, rebounding, quickness, jumping, moves around the basket, defense around the basket, conditioning and teamwork.

RED JENKINS
W.T. Woodson High School, Fairfax, Virginia

In 17 years at Woodson High School, Red Jenkins' record is 270-107. This includes eight district championships in 14 years in league. In 1977 Coach Jenkins was named Virginia Basketball Coach of the Year, Region III Coach of the Year, and was also one of the eight finalists for National Coach of the Year. In 1967 and 1975 he was honored as Northern Region Coach of the Year. He has coached in the McDonalds' Capital Classic, in the Capital All Stars game against the Russian Junior Olympic Team, in the McDonalds' East-West All-Star game, and in the Dapper Dan Classic in Pittsburgh (winning all four).

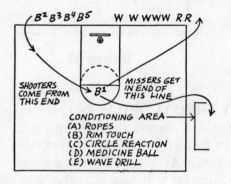

Diagram 54

WOODSON'S 1 PLUS 1 DRILL: Our 1 + 1 drill is the "pressure" phase of our three part system. All team members line up on the baseline after practice (before conditioning). B1 shoots foul in bonus situations. If he makes *both* ends, he is "out" of the game and goes to conditioning. If he misses the first, everyone (blues, whites, reds) run one sprint (down and back in 10 seconds). If he makes the first and misses the second, everyone runs half sprint. Any shooter who misses either one must get in the end of the line and run on all misses. Generally we let everyone shoot once (12 men). We sometimes let just blues shoot (after a good practice) or just whites or sometimes we just pick out players at random. After everyone gets accustomed to the drill and realizes its game importance, we run a full sprint on second shot misses and two full sprints on first shot misses.

Special Value of the Drill: This drill puts pressure on our foul shooters to perform. It offers reward for success and additional work for failure. It is a serious drill for us as we have been over 70% for five straight years.

DICK KUCHEN
University of California, Berkeley

Dick Kuchen is the head basketball coach at the University of California. After establishing many rebounding and scoring records at Rider College in New Jersey, he had a brief career in the NBA, spent one year playing in the European League, and served one season as basketball coach at Art Institute J.C. in Pittsburgh, Pa. He then moved to Washington University in Missouri before going to Iowa University in 1970. There he remained for three seasons before going to Notre Dame as an assistant to Digger Phelps for three seasons. While at Notre Dame, he was assigned the role of coaching the big men on the Irish squad.

WEAKSIDE MOVEMENT DRILL: This drill has been extremely valuable in working on our moves without the ball. Diagram 55A: We fill the point, wing, and corner. A coach fills the wing area and acts as a fourth offensive player. Diagram 55B: 01 passes the ball to the coach and screens away; 02 down screens for 03; 03 takes depth to the baseline and runs an interior cut.

Diagram 55C: 01 continues to screen to the baseline for 02; 02 comes to the point position; 01 screens for 03 who comes to the wing. It is important for each offensive player to visualize a defensive player and set his pick accordingly. We also work on V cuts on all baseline screens. I think this drill gives offside offensive players an idea of how important a role they can play in the offense. The coach can end the drill at any time by passing inside or he can create a court reversal. This keeps pressure on all offensive players to move to their spots.

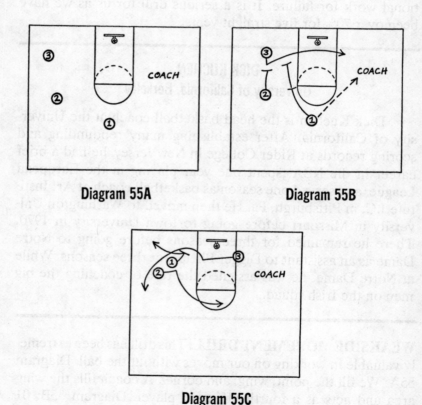

Diagram 55A   **Diagram 55B**

Diagram 55C

Part II

DEFENSIVE DRILLS

BERT JENKINS
Gulfport High School, Gulfport, Mississippi

After spending ten years at Gulfport Junior High School in Gulfport, Mississippi, Bert Jenkins moved to Gulfport High School. In 18 seasons there he recorded a remarkable 579 wins against only 102 losses. Included in this are 12 District 8 Championships, 9 "Big 8" Conference Championships, 4 "AA" State Championships, and 3 Overall State Championships. A frequent lecturer at basketball coaching clinics, Coach Jenkins has been named Mississippi "Coach of the Year" on three occasions and twice has been afforded the honor of Southeast Region (11 states) "Coach of the Year."

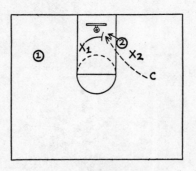

Diagram 56A

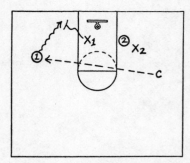

Diagram 56B

ADMIRAL DRILL: In Diagram 56A, X1, in help position from the ball, helps defend against the lob pass by the coach to 2 by attempting to pick off the pass or trying to draw the charge.

In Diagram 56B, X1 hustles to cover his man who receives a cross court pass and tries to draw the charge. 1 can only drive baseline after he receives the pass.

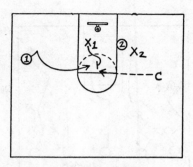

Diagram 56C

In Diagram 56C, X1 sees his man cutting to the ball and beats him to the spot.

Special Value of the Drill: This drill helps to teach defensive play on the man off the ball two or more passes away. It teaches the three duties in our man-to-man defense. The coach can pass the lob to the low post, the cross court pass to 1, or signal 1 to cut to the ball. X1 learns to handle all three situations.

VINCE SCHAEFER
Miami Senior High School, Miami, Florida

Chosen as the National High School Basketball Coach of the Year, Vince Schaefer has been the Head Basketball Coach and Athletic Director at Miami Senior High School for 40 years. During that time his teams have won 704 games while losing only 187. He has won 5 State High School basketball championships. He is the first and only high school coach to receive the Award of Merit from the National Association of Basketball Coaches of the United States. Coach Schaefer organized and has twice coached in the Florida North-South All Star game.

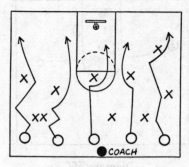

Diagram 57

BEAT-THE-SCREEN DRILL: The best way to beat screens is
to know where they are and to try to avoid running into them
by stepping around them. In the beat-the-screen drill a group
of players is stationed at random across the floor. Another
group uses good defensive footwork to gradually back up and
slide through the screens on signals from the coach.

DICK HARTER
Penn State University

Dick Harter earned three basketball letters at Penn, helping the Quakers win the Ivy League title. He became the basketball coach at the Germantown Academy in Philadelphia for two
years. He was 16-9 in his only season at Rider, then turned
around Penn's program in his five years at the Philadelphia
school, compiling a 53-3 record and qualifying for the NCAA
tournament in 1970 and 1971. His first Oregon team was 6-20,
but he then led the Ducks to six straight winning seasons and
three tournament bids. Harter has taken his teams to post-
season tournaments five of the last 10 years and his teams have
won nine tournament or conference titles. He was named NCAA
District 2 Coach of the Year in 1971 and Eastern Coach of the
Year the same season by the Philadelphia Basketball Writers.
He was also honored as Pac-8 Coach of the Year in 1977.

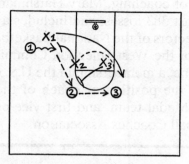

Diagram 58

CHECK AND ROTATION DRILL: O1 drives to inside of the court. X1 allows drive. X2 makes a defensive check on the drive. O1 passes to O2 and forces X3 to make a defensive switch. O2 passes to O3 and X1 must pick him up. When the ball gets to O3 it becomes a 3-on-3 game. O1, O2, and O3 look to score at any point in the drill if they are not played hard.

Special Value of the Drill: Good man-to-man defense is based on the coordination and teamwork between the five defensive players on the floor. The check and rotation drill demands teamwork, talking, and effort.

MARV HARSHMAN
University of Washington

In 13 years at Pacific Lutheran University, Coach Harshman compiled a record of 241 wins against 121 losses. This included 7 conference championships, 1 second place finish and 2 thirds. During this time they participated in 5 national tournaments. Following his tenure at Pacific Lutheran he spent 13 seasons at Washington State University. He then moved to the University of Washington, where in 8 years he recorded 133 wins against 81 losses. His 1976 team participated in the NCAA Tournament.

In 34 years of coaching, Marv Harshman's record stands at 529 wins against 383 losses, and includes a membership on the Board of Directors of the National Basketball Hall of Fame, a chairmanship of the West Selection Committee in the East-West All Star game, a membership in the U.S. Olympic Basketball Committee, the position of coach of the 1975 U.S. Pan American Gold Medal team, and first vice-presidency of the National Basketball Coaches Association.

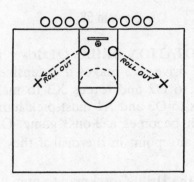

Diagram 59

CLOSE OUT DRILL: In this close out drill the squad is divided into two groups. The man with the ball stands under the basket, rolls it to partner located on the side, slides out to the man on the baseline side. Players must be taught to slide out with short steps and contain the player with the ball. The attack comes from the baseline side and the offensive player is forced to defensive help in the center. When the shot is taken the defensive player blocks out and goes to the board. Players continue to alternate sides.

Special Value of the Drill: The drill teaches players to get back to man when sagging on weak side defense. Players learn to close out on the shooter and to contain the man while driving him away from the baseline. Gives players practice cutting shooter out after the shot.

BILL FOSTER
Clemson University

Bill Foster began his career as the Freshman coach at Carson-Newman College in 1957 where his team was 19-1. He then moved to Marion High School and recorded a 42-21 record. He spent six years at Shorter College in Georgia during which he compiled a record of 110-31. In 1967 he accepted a position as assistant coach at The Citadel and from there he moved to North Carolina-Charlotte. In five years his teams were 88-39. In 1975 he accepted his present position at Clemson University. His Clemson teams have posted 74 wins against 38 losses. Currently, his college total of 272-108 and 17-year record of 333-130 distinguishes him as the 9th winningest active college coach.

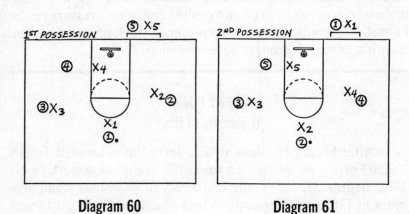

Diagram 60   Diagram 61

COMPETITIVE SHELL DRILL: The *Shell Drill* is a man-to-man defensive drill in a game type situation. The squad is divided into three teams during the opening days of practice and a season-long round robin tournament decides the "shell champion."

The game is played 4-on-4 in the half court. Play begins with (A) a dribble across the half court line or (B) a throw in from out-of-bounds. Teams A and B have the ball for five possessions each with one point given to the *defensive* team for each basket the offense scores. The coaches call fouls and violations, and a daily point total is recorded with the team accumulating the *fewest* points during the season declared the champions. To encourage players to take charging fouls, the defense gets a point subtracted from the total for each charging foul called.

While teams A and B play, team C is on the other end shooting free throws.

Special Value of the Drill: The drill is the favorite among the players because it is very competitive — there is a winner and loser every day.

Every defensive situation that you will face in a game occurs in this drill. Whether yours is a sagging defense or a deny defense, "Shell" enables you as a coach to teach how to get the players to react to each offensive situation. Peer pressure tends to motivate a weaker defensive player to work harder when he is with a group of stronger defensive men.

JERRY PIMM
University of Utah

After his playing days at USC Jerry Pimm assisted Trojan coach Forrest Twogood for a year while completing work on his M.A. degree. He joined the University of Utah basketball program in 1961 as an assistant to Jack Gardner. During his years as an assistant, Utah made two NCAA post season appearances and traveled three times to the NIT. In 1974 he took over as the head coach at Utah. Since that time he has compiled a record of 101-40 for a .716 winning percentage. He won a WAC Championship in 1977 and finished second three times. Pimm was named District Seven "Coach of the Year" in 1976 and 1977 and was third in the National "Coach of the Year" balloting in 1977. In 1977 he was named Utah's "Sportsman of the Year."

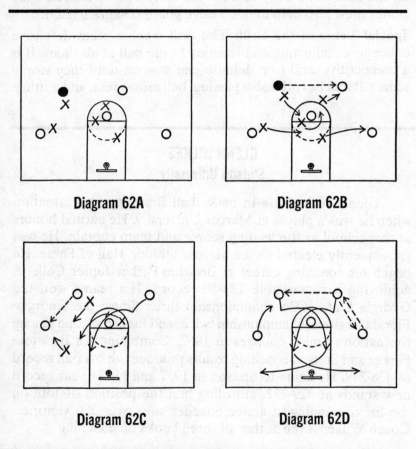

Diagram 62A   Diagram 62B

Diagram 62C   Diagram 62D

DEFENSIVE ADJUSTMENT DRILL: The drill starts with the offense set up in two guard — 2 forward — center alignment. As the ball is moved around the outside (no skipping) the defense adjusts with each pass (Diagrams 62A and 62B). After ball has been moved from corner to corner several times, the opposite guard cuts off the high post screen after the ball reaches the corner. The cutter continues through and out to his same side if he doesn't receive a pass. The ball is then swung around to the opposite corner and the other guard cuts off the high post. The drill is continuous. The defensive guard must shoot off the cutter and deny through the lane. The defender on the center must also help the defensive guard (Diagram 62D).

Special Value of the Drill: The drill teaches team defensive concepts of adjusting and reacting to the ball at all times. It is a competitive drill (the defense can stay on until they stop a score). It teaches offensive passing, ball movement, and cutting.

GLENN WILKES
Stetson University

Glenn Wilkes' life in basketball first attracted attention when he was a player at Mercer University. He earned honors at that school as the leading scorer and team captain. He was subsequently elected to the Mercer athletic Hall of Fame. He began his coaching career at Brewton-Parker Junior College, achieving a remarkable 123-30 record. His teams won the Georgia State JuCo championship three times; the Georgia-Florida Regional championship twice; and ranked second among the nation's junior colleges in 1957. Combining his Brewton-Parker and Stetson coaching results produces an over-all record of 438-249. He came to Stetson in 1957 and his 21 year record now stands at 329-232, affording him the position of 13th on the list of winningest active coaches with over 300 victories. Coach Wilkes is the author of three books on coaching.

DEFENSIVE RECOVERY DRILL: The coach makes a long pass down-court to another coach or a manager. The defensive team (X) retreats as quickly as possible and sets up in designated defense. The coach can designate the defense in advance or have a defensive quarterback call the defense while retreating down-court. The coach who receives the pass may shoot the ball, drive, or pass to one of the offensive players (O). The drill continues until the defense gets the ball. Defensive players may not line up even with their own man.

Emphasize: 1. Full speed defensive recovery.
2. Defensive talk.
3. Retreat to the line of the ball.
4. Ball side of the floor.
5. Defensive rebound.

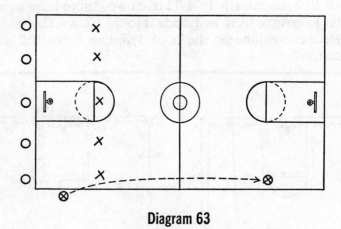

Diagram 63

Special Value of the Drill: The drill teaches defensive recovery in game-type situation. It can be used to work on changing defenses. It teaches ball-side defense and defensive rebounding from the transition game.

CHUCK SMITH
University of Missouri — St. Louis

In the 1950's Charles "Chuck" Smith coached high school teams in the southern Missouri towns of Leadwood and Boone Terre. The teams responded by winning more than 70% of their games. In 1959 he left the high school ranks for the head coaching job at Washington University. In six years, he compiled an 84-59 record, including an outstanding 21-6 record in 1964. The following year he left for Central Missouri State University where his only team finished 14-8, second in the Missouri Intercollegiate Athletic Association. In 1966 the University of Missoui — St. Louis launched an intercollegiate athletic program, and Chuck Smith was the person named to organize it. He has produced outstanding individuals, including three UMSL All-Americans. He coached USML's 1968-69 finalists term to a 19-7 record. His 1971-72 team won more games than any other Riverman team and made it to the NCAA Division II finals. He has co-authored the book *Winning Basketball* with Gene Bartow.

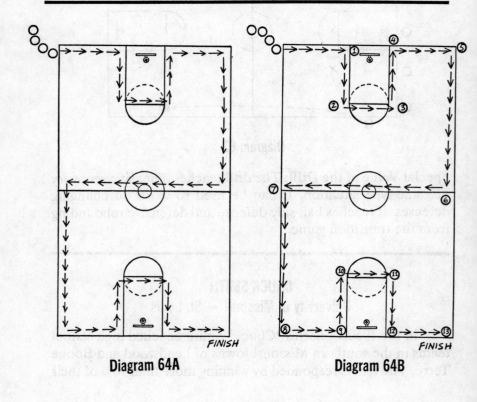

FINISH   FINISH

Diagram 64A   **Diagram 64B**

DEFENSIVE SLIDE DRILL: In Diagram 64A the players take a defensive stance and slide laterally. At each junction of lines they change direction but continue the lateral defensive sliding movement. The next player in line waits until the player in front of him comes to the first junction before starting his sliding.

In Diagram 64B: the players slide laterally to Junction 1, retreat steps to Junction 2, slide laterally to Junction 3, retreat steps to Junction 4, slide laterally to Junction 5, approach steps to Junction 6, slide laterally to Junction 7, retreat steps to Junction 8, slide laterally to Junction 9, retreat steps to Junction 10, slide laterally to Junction 11, retreat steps to Junction 12, and slide laterally to Junction 13 and the finish.

Special Value of the Drill: The drill helps develop change of direction defensive steps and slides applicable to game conditions.

KENT SMITH
Boulder High School, Boulder, Colorado

Kent Smith is the Varsity Basketball Coach at Boulder High School. In eight years he has compiled a 156-36 record, including 4 District Championships, 4 Division Championships, 3 League Championships, and 2 State Championships. Five of his eight teams have been in the State Tournament with a 7th place in 1972, 4th place in 1975, 5th place in 1976, and State Titles in 1977 and 1979. Prior coaching experience was at East Junior High School in Aurora, Colorado, and Aurora Central High School. Coach Smith was selected "Coach of the Year" in 1977 in Colorado. He also coached the South All-State Team in 1975, and the Denver Metro All Stars in 1977 for the Cactus Classic in Albuquerque. He is the author of *Winning Basketball with the Multiple Motion Offense.*

DENY AND HELP DRILL: The coach plays the point guard to control the drill as he wishes. On one side of the basket, defenders X1 and X2 work against players A and B. These players screen down for each other so that X1 and X2 can work on going over the screen and still keep denial pressure on the pass from the point. They must also guard against backdoor cuts. Defender X3 works on denial of pass if coach brings the ball to that side of the floor, or jumps to helpside position to prevent backdoor cuts (or takes the charge if the pass is successfully made). This drill must be run hard to simulate game speed action. Defender X3 always jumps to helpside position when the coach dribbles or passes away from the man he is guarding.

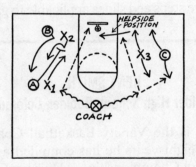

Diagram 65

Special Value of the Drill: The drill allows you to create game situations to defend at game speeds. This is especially necessary if you play pressure man-to-man defense. A real key to being successful when playing man-to-man defense is preventing layups. This drill allows your players to work against screens, guard-forward pass denial, and helpside position to take the charge or prevent layups.

RALPH BALL
Princeton High School, Princeton, West Virginia

During 20 seasons as head basketball coach at Princeton High School, Ralph Ball has achieved a 60% winning record. This includes seven area championships, five Coalfield Conference Championships, and one West Virginia AAA State Championship. He was named "Coach of the Year" in the state in 1978-79.

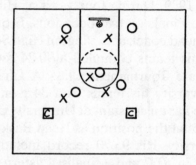

Diagram 66

DENY DRILL: The purpose of the drill is to deny the ball to the offense. The defense must stay between his man and the ball at all times. The two coaches are part of the offense. They pass the ball between each other and they pass to the offense, who in turn try to score. The coaches may move to various positions on the floor (there is no defense on the coaches). You can let the players stay on offense as long as they score. The defense must take the ball away from them. The coach should have penalties for scoring or offensive rebounding.

Special Value of the Drill: The drill teaches overplay on the ball side and sag on the helpside. Every time the ball is passed between the coaches, it requires the defense to adjust their positions. It is more demanding than regular defensive game conditions with the two coaches passing the ball.

ROLLIE MASSIMINO
Villanova University

Rollie Massimino began his coaching career as an assistant at Cranford High School. He moved to Hillside High School as a head coach in 1959. During four years at Hillside his teams went to the State Finals on two occasions. From 1963 to 1969 he served as the head coach at Lexington High School in Massachusetts where his teams compiled a 90-34 record. His team won the Bay State Tournament Class A Championship. At Stonybrook University his teams won 34 games while losing 16. He then served as an assistant at University of Pennsylvania. In 1973 he accepted the position as Head Basketball Coach at Villanova University. His 93-70 record includes a 3rd place finish in the NIT in 1977 and a finalist Eastern Regional finish in 1978. Through eight years of college coaching his record stands at 127 wins and 96 losses. He won 160 of 221 games in his high school coaching career.

FORWARD ADJUSTMENT DRILL: This is a two-man defensive drill designed to work on defensive positioning of the two forwards. Depending on where the ball is located, the two defensive players must move accordingly. With the ball on the top left side with O1, X1 is in a denial position, preventing O2 from receiving the ball. X2 is in a help position to stop the back door pass. If O1 passes the ball to O3, X2 now moves to a denial position while X1 takes a help position. In this drill the ball is reversed back and forth so that the two defensive players really have to work on denying and then quickly getting in the help position.

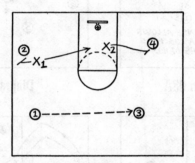

Diagram 67

Special Value of the Drill: In this drill you are teaching your forwards the importance of denial and then getting to the help position as the ball is moved around. It simulates game conditions and helps to establish good defensive habits.

JERRY KRAUSE
Eastern Washington University

J.V. "Jerry" Krause's record at Eastern is 209-141 and his overall record is 347-199. He coached at the high school level from 1959 through 1964 in Adair, Iowa, and Loveland, Colorado. He also served as the assistant basketball coach at Northern Colorado for two years before coming to Eastern Washington in 1967. Eastern's basketball program compiled three tournament championships, two Evergreen Conference titles, one conference co-championship, an undefeated conference season, a 16-game win streak, and an NAIA District I playoff berth. He was Northwest Small College Coach of the Year for 1976.

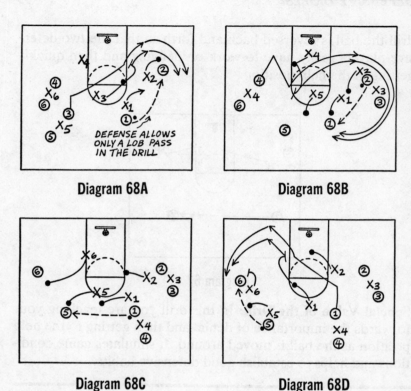

DEFENSE ALLOWS
ONLY A LOB PASS
IN THE DRILL

Diagram 68A   **Diagram 68B**

Diagram 68C   **Diagram 68D**

4-ON-4 BLOOD ALLEY (12 players are needed): Purpose of
the Drill: Defending "front" cuts (cuts made by the offensive
player between their man and the ball) as well as practicing
defensive "position" and "communication" skills. The drill is
designed to give players concentrated work on the technique of
denying front cuts made from different positions on the floor.
We try never to allow a front cut, i.e., we maintain a BALL-
YOU-MAN relationship at all times.

Diagram 68A — Pass from O1 to O2 (guard to forward).
All defenders "explode" to new defensive position. O3 attempts
a front cut in blood alley (free throw lane). X3 defends the cut.
O3 and X3 will now rotate out opposite and O5 and X5 will
rotate in.

Diagram 68B — Pass from O2 to O1 (forward to guard). O4 attempts front cut as X4 defends. O4 and X4 rotate cut opposite and O6 and X6 rotate in.

Diagram 68C — Pass from O1 to O5 (guard to guard). All defenders explode to new defensive position. There are no cuts.

Diagram 68D — Pass from O5 to O6. Same as in Diagram 68A.

Special Value of the Drill: As the ball is passed from side to side, players receive concentrated work on denying "front" cuts as well as practicing many other defensive techniques, i.e., positioning with relationship to the ball and man, communication, "exploding" to the ball, inside defensive techniques on cutters, etc.

BUD PRESLEY
Menlo College

When Bud Presley came to Menlo College in 1971, the Oaks had won only 11 games in the previous four seasons. Menlo has since won 187 games while losing but 36.

Bud Presley has a national reputation as a defensive specialist. He has served as consultant coach to the 1972 Australian Olympic team, as defensive consultant to the Golden State Warriors, and as a scout for the Portland Trail Blazers. In 28 years of coaching, his name has become synonymous with highly intense and aggressive defense, and deliberate, precision-drill offense.

Coach Presley was Coast Conference and California Community College Small Division "Coach of the Year" in 1974.

4-ON-4 DEFENSIVE HELP DRILL: In Diagram 69A, G1 penetrates with a hard dribble to inside; O2 helps (delays ball), then jumps back to G2 as ball is passed out; O1 recovers G1. Now G2 drives inside on O2; O4 (defensive forward) jumps to ball and then closes out on F4 as ball is passed out. Ball now

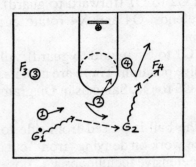

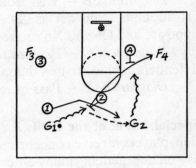

Diagram 69A   Diagram 69B

starts back around horn with F4 penetrating over the top and O2 helping and recovering. The drill is continued until two full rotations have been made.

In Diagram 69B the same drill (penetration of ball around horn) is repeated, but this time players switch by calling "Cross," simulating a situation in which no recovery is possible. In a game, the helper always decides whether to "cross" or help and recover.

Special Value of the Drill: Teaches when and how to "help and recover" and/or "cross" (switch) in a dribble penetration situation. It also reinforces help calls and defensive man-ball relationships.

ERNIE WHEELER
California Polytechnic State University — San Luis Obispo

In seven seasons as head basketball coach at Magnolia High School in Anaheim, California, Ernie Wheeler compiled 133 wins against 55 losses. From there he moved to Cal Poly University in San Luis Obispo as the Freshman coach. In two seasons he recorded 41 wins against only 8 losses. In 1972 he became the head coach. In eight seasons at the helm he has won 132 games while losing 79. His teams have won three conference championships and were Western Regional Champions in 1976-77. In 6 of his 8 years his teams have been ranked in the top 10 in the nation on defense. They were ranked #1 in defense in the nation in 1974-75. He has been named "Coach of the Year" on three occasions and was District 6, 7, and 8 "Coach of the Year" in 1976-77.

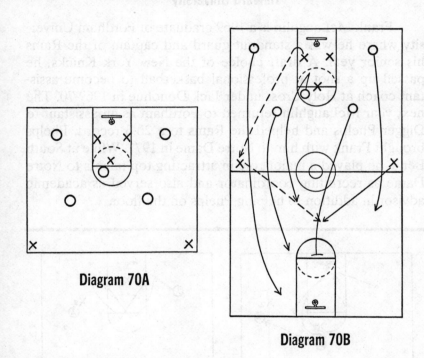

Diagram 70A

Diagram 70B

"GET BACK" DRILL: This drill is designed to teach players to recover as a *team* and take away the opponents' fast break. Three defensive players take a position in a triangle under the basket. Two defensive players are at half-court on the sideline on each side. The five offensive players make from three to five passes and then take a shot. The defense makes an outlet pass to half-court. The half-court man hits the opposite man on the sideline for an attempted layup. Five defensive men must now get back and stop the layup. If the layup is scored, the defensive team must run laps. *Note:* All players must stay in their offensive position. No one can release until the *rebound.* This is a very important coaching point.

FRANK McLAUGHLIN
Harvard University

Frank McLaughlin is a 1969 graduate of Fordham University where he was a standout guard and captain of the Rams his senior year. A draft choice of the New York Knicks, he passed up a shot at professional basketball to become assistant coach at Holy Cross under Jack Donohue in 1969-70. The next year McLaughlin returned to Fordham as an assistant to Digger Phelps and helped the Rams to a 23-6 record. Phelps brought Frank with him to Notre Dame in 1971. While at South Bend, he played a major role in attracting top talents to Notre Dame as recruiting coordinator and also served as academic advisor in addition to helping Phelps on the floor.

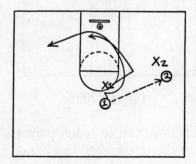

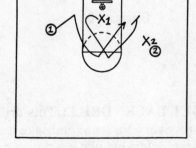

Diagram 71A   Diagram 71B

GIVE AND GO/FLASH PIVOT/POST DEFENSE: 1 passes to 2 and tries to cut to the basket. X2 allows the first pass. X1 jumps into the path of the cutter and does not allow 1 to cut between him and the ball. 1 moves to the opposite side after the cut. X1 assumes a weakside help position. X2 now pressures the passer, #2. 1 tries to cut low first and then attempts to flash high post for a pass from 2. X1 denies by overplaying 1 in all his attempts to receive the pass from 2.

Special Value of the Drill: The drill teaches cut defense, weakside help position, and flash pivot and post defense. It also teaches good passing and offensive movement.

FRAN WEBSTER
University of Pittsburgh

Since Fran Webster was named to the Pitt staff as an assistant coach in charge of defense, he has built Pitt's defense into one of the most intricate, bewildering and successful in the nation. His creation, a constantly-changing combination of zone and man-to-man, was nicknamed the "Amoeba" Defense by an opposing coach because, like an amoeba, it never looks the same for very long. Along with his defensive duties, Webster is in charge of breaking down game films, statistics, and other administrative and academic affairs concerning the players. He joined former Coach Buzz Ridl's staff at Pitt after serving as Ridl's assistant coach for five years at Westminster College. Prior to this he had 10 highly successful years as head coach at Hickory (Pa.) High School. During his tenure there he directed the school to five county championships and its first Western Regional Class A title when the team went to the state finals in 1961.

JUMP-SWITCH DRILL: This drill gives the players practice in executing the jump-switch properly. The player guarded by the No. 1 defensive player dribbles and the No. 2 makes the jump-switch. No. 1 moves down the floor. No. 2 forces the dribbler toward No. 1, then No. 1 jump switches. This continues the length of the court. To give the players the proper practice, the dribbler stops when the jump-switch is made. At the center and at the completion of the drill at the end of the court, they also practice the double-team move. The player making the jump-switch shouts "go" in the middle of his move. This enables the other defensive player to start his move down court sooner.

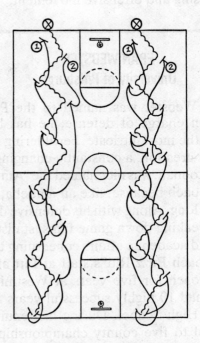

Diagram 72

Special Value of the Drill: The jump-switch, fake jump-switch, and double team are very important moves in both our man-to-man and zone defenses. This drill helps the players to learn the basic fundamentals necessary for a successful jump-switch or double-team.

BRUCE PARKHILL
College of William and Mary

Bruce Parkhill is a 1971 graduate of Lock Haven State College. At the University of Virginia, he earned his masters and also served as graduate assistant coach for the Cavaliers. He then spent 5 seasons as an assistant at William and Mary before becoming the youngest head coach in major college basketball in 1977. In 1977 the College of William and Mary won the Cougar Classic at BYU and the Tangerine Bowl Classic, while posting the best won-lost percentage in 15 years at the school. Last season Coach Parkhill was the recipient of the Collegiate Basketball Officials Association Sportsmanship Award for the greater Washington area, designed to go to the college "which best exemplified the highest degree of sportsmanship, character and ethics among its players and coaches."

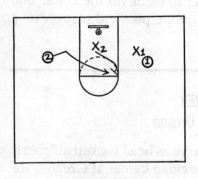

Diagram 73A

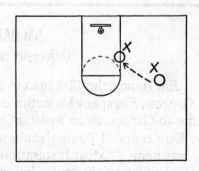

Diagram 73B

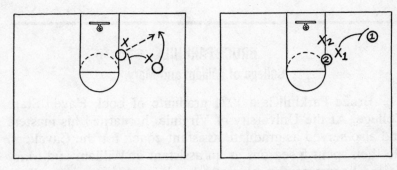

Diagram 73C   Diagram 73D

POST SUPPORT DRILL: In this "post support" drill, O1 is positioned on the wing with his dribble used. X1 is playing O1 tight in order to pressure pass. O2 is on the weakside and flashes to the strongside post. X2 is in a help position and meets O2 in the lane to bump him high and ballside fronts. O1 then passes into O2. X1 drops off O1 and digs into the post. O2 makes a move to score or passes out to O1. X1 then has to recover to O1.

Special Value of the Drill: The drill teaches offense to pass under pressure, weakside defender to block off the cutter, and perimeter defensive man to help on the post and recover on a pass out.

JIM HANEY
University of Oregon

Jim Haney, the 12th man to serve as head basketball coach at Oregon, has spent his entire coaching career at Oregon. He came to Oregon as an assistant in 1971, after graduation from the University of Pennsylvania where he earned three letters. He was named "Most Inspirational Flyer" on the 1970-71 team that won 28 straight games before losing in the NCAA Eastern Regional. At the age of 29 he became the youngest head basketball coach in the Pac-10. But his seven years on the staff — the last two as chief assistant — have made him a proven veteran of top-level collegiate basketball campaigns.

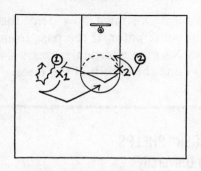

Diagram 74A

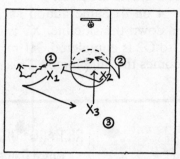

Diagram 74B

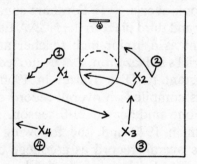

Diagram 74C

PRESS DRILLS:

   2 on 2: O1 dribbles to sidelines; X1 forces sideline and turns O1. X2 overplays O2; X2 gets off his man as O1 nears sideline. X2 anticipates O1 turn; X2 jumps O1, running at O1 in the passing lane, forcing a lob or bounce pass; X1 turns O1 and leaves immediately and picks up O2. O2 now dribbles to other sideline; X1 and X2 repeat the process. This is done in groups of four the length of the floor.

3 on 3: O1, O2, X1, X2 do the same as 2 on 2. O3 stays in the middle of the court opposite the ball. X3 stays ball side of O3 and anticipates the pass from O1 to O2. If the pass is completed from O1 to O2, X1 picks up X3 man. This is done the length of the floor.

4 on 4: Same action as 3 on 3. X4 must now deny the pass down the sideline. X3 is the anticipator. If the pass from O1 to O2 is completed, X1 takes X3 man and denies pass; X4 becomes the anticipator. This is done the length of the floor.

RICHARD "DIGGER" PHELPS
Notre Dame University

"Digger" Phelps first gained the attention of the basketball world when he took over a 10-15 Fordham squad and finished with a 26-3 ledger and third place in the NCAA Eastern Regional. After a brief stint as a junior high teacher and high school coach at St. Gabriel's in Hazelton, Pa., he moved on to Pennsylvania as an assistant to Dick Harter in 1966. As freshman coach, his squads compiled an overall record of 65-20 in four years, including one undefeated 21-0 season. From there he went to Fordham in 1970 and, the following year, came to Notre Dame. His overall record as a college coach is 206-81 for a .718 victory mark. He has taken eight teams to NCAA tournaments and led his team to the NCAA tournament each of the last seven years. In 1978 he guided the Irish to the final four of the NCAA tournament and in 1979 they advanced to the Regional Championship before losing to the eventual NCAA Champion Michigan State Spartans.

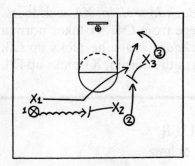

Diagram 75A

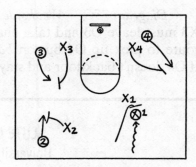

Diagram 75B

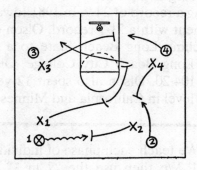

Diagram 75C

ROTATION PRESS:

Diagram 75A — Guards — Forward Commitment: X1 will force O1 into the middle with a dribble. X2 releases to charge at O1. X1 releases O1 to X2 and drops back to help in the middle. If X3 picks up O2 and releases O3, X1 must pick up O3.

Diagram 75B — Shutout 4 on 4: O1 will pick up the dribble with X1 pressuring the ball. All others must loosen up to the ball and deny all passing lanes.

Diagram 75C — Weakside Backdoor Help: X4 backdoors. X3 must leave O3 and take charge from O4. X1 takes normal route to pick up O4 but on *backdoor move* he picks up O3. If O4 doesn't backdoor and stays in the corner, X1 picks up O4.

LUTE OLSON
University of Iowa

Lute Olson was selected National "Coach of the Year" in 1980 after leading Iowa to the final four of the NCAA tournament and posting a record of 24-9. In 1981 Iowa returned to the NCAA tournament with a 21-7 record. Olson came to Iowa in 1974 after coaching Long Beach State to a 24-2 season. As head coach at Long Beach City College, Olson had a four-year record of 104-20. Olson also spent 12 years coaching at the high school level in California and Minnesota.

7-IN-1 DRILL: We teach each phase of individual defense in a breakdown drill. We then use the "7 in 1" drill to give us constant review of the techniques we want our players to employ. We also use a pantomine situation with two players at each of the six baskets working without the ball to get as much review as possible in a short period of time.

Individual Drills:
   A. *Pressure the Lead Pass:* The offensive man drives baseline when he receives the pass. The defender cuts him off and then yells "dead" to indicate to his teammates that the dribbler has terminated his dribble. The offensive man holds the ball over his head for a count of two and then returns the ball to the coach. He then tries to create another lead. The defender goes to offense only after deflecting or stealing the pass. The next player (X2) becomes the defender.

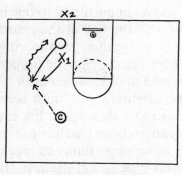

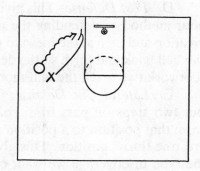

Diagram 76A   **Diagram 76B**

B. *Cut off the Driver and Pressure the Passer:* Here you teach the proper retreat and baseline cutoff. After the "dead" call, the defender pressures the passer.

C. *Backdoor Coverage:* The defender attempts to deny the lead (if he does not, the ball is thrown to the receiver and continue as in drill 1 and 2). If the man is denied the lead, then he will break on a backdoor cut at which time the proper coverage is taught (we turn with him, throwing the trail hand and arm into the passing lane). The coach throws the ball to get the defender to react.

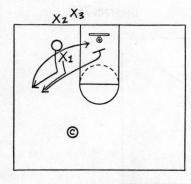

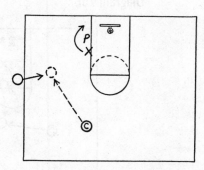

Diagram 76C   **Diagram 76D**

D. *Post Defense:* This gives you an opportunity to teach your method of defending the post with the ball at the guard position and then at the forward position. We then go to moving the ball back and forth so the defender can develop the proper footwork (we teach the half-moon method of post defense).

E. *Lateral Cut Defense:* The offensive post must step out two steps on pass from coach to O2, then make his cut from that position to a position anywhere from baseline to the 3rd free throw position. This gives us an opportunity to teach the type of coverage we want on this type of cut (flash post) as well as getting him off the man when he has gone from ball-side to helpside position.

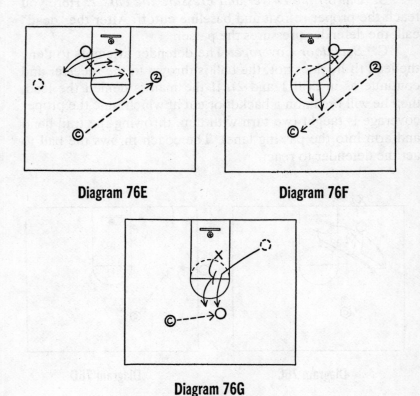

Diagram 76E   **Diagram 76F**

Diagram 76G

F. *Diagonal Cut Defense:* The offense must again take two steps out before he starts the cut. This occurs when O2 passes back to the coach. The defender jumps to the ball and establishes proper ball-man position and then forces the offensive player *outside of the circle.*

G. *One-on-one:* After forcing the offensive player out of the circle area, the defender will now play him one-on-one with normal on ball defensive rules applying (the offensive player is limited to two dribbles). This includes dictating direction, pressuring the shooter and blocking out.

The individual drills are then combined into a "7-in-1" Drill which gives us a ten minute review of our basic off-ball and on-ball responsibilities.

BOB FULLER
Highland High School, Anderson, Indiana

Bob Fuller's 17-year span as a high school coach produced an overall record of 347 wins against 89 losses, including 21 tournament championships and 14 conference titles. He coached at Shabbona High School and Elgin High School (in Illinois) and North Judson High School (Indiana) and Highland High School in Anderson, Indiana. He has been named "Coach of the Year" on 10 occasions. He wrote *Basketball's Wishbone Offense* and *Basketball's Man-Zone Defense.*

7-ON-5 GET BACK DRILL: The X's (defensive fast break team) run their various offensive options. If they score they get the ball again at mid-court. If a field goal attempt is missed or the defense (the numbers) recovers the ball by a rebound or an interception, the X's immediately retreat to defense, and the initial defensive team (the numbers) fast breaks to the opposite end of the floor. The fast break team has an added advantage because as soon as the ball changes hands, numbers 6 and 7 (who are on opposite sidelines from each other at mid-court) quickly sprint to the other end of the floor and join the other five numbered players in a 7 on 5 fast break. Make a pressure simulated, competitive game out of it by keeping score:

X's score = basket (1 point), free throw (1 point), offensive rebound (1 point), stop fast break attempt (1 point).

O's score = drawing a foul (5 points), scoring on fast break (5 points), and offensive rebound (1 point).

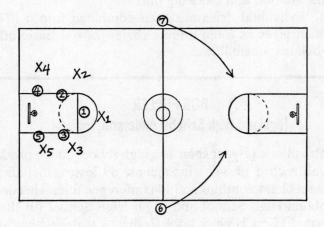

Diagram 77

Special Value of the Drill:
1. An excellent drill to practice stopping the in-bounds pass, pressing the rebounder, stopping the outlet pass and other defensive fast break specifics.
2. Excellent conditioning drill as play is continuous.
3. Drill provides pressure simulated game-like experience.
4. All shooting (including free throws) is under pressure.
5. Teaches not to make foolish fouls.
6. Strengthens both blocking out and offensive rebounding skills.

TOM APKE
University of Colorado

Tom Apke began his career at Creighton as a scholarship basketball player. Following graduation, he served as a graduate assistant coach at the University of Cincinnati. He then spent two seasons as basketball coach at McNicholas High School in the same city, then returned to Creighton. He was an assistant under his former coach, then served under Eddie Sutton for five years before succeeding him in 1974. His mark at Creighton is 93-43, a .684 winning percentage. He is fourth in wins among all-time Creighton coaches. His teams participated in three NCAA Tournaments and one NIT. He has been named "Coach of the Year" in the Missouri Valley Conference and District Five "Coach of the Year" by the National Association of Basketball Coaches. Tom became Colorado's head coach in 1981.

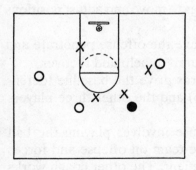

Diagram 78A

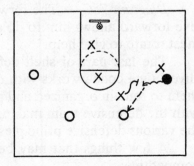

Diagram 78B

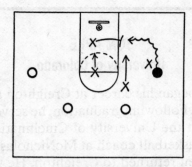

Diagram 78C

SHELL DEFENSE: If we were allowed only one defensive drill, this would be the one that I would choose. It is without a doubt our best drill: it teaches all our defensive principles in a learning situation and it is competitive so that our players work hard; it has the side benefit of helping as an offensive drill as well. We start out with two guards and two forwards and work with them because their defensive responsibilities seldom change when there is a post man present; sometimes we add the center.

Diagram 78A — In the first part of the shell, we keep the offense stationary. The defense has to move and adjust positions on the court as the ball is passed.

Diagram 78B — Next we have the offense penetrate and pitch so that the defense has to learn to help and recover.

Diagram 78C — The forwards drive the baseline (defensive forward allows him to do so) and the other three players must rotate to give help.

The last part of shell defense involves playing the ball "live." One coach works with the team on offense and forces them to remain organized and patient. The other coach works with the defensive team making sure that his players all apply the various defensive principles.

A few things that may be done to make the drill more competitive:

    1. We play "live" shell to four or five baskets alternating possession of the ball by each team; winners get a

drink and losers have to run a couple of laps. This makes them play hard and concentrate. It has the added benefit of showing us who responds well when the game is on the line and who doesn't play as well in a pressure situation.

2. We also fast break from this situation occasionally. This helps our players concentrate on defense because they can get the ball back if they stop the other team. It also encourages blocking out, which many defensive drills do not.

GENE BESS
Three Rivers Community College

Gene Bess's coaching career began at Lesterville High School in Missouri, and he then moved to Anniston (Mo.) High School. In 1965 he accepted the head job at Oran (Mo.) High School. In five seasons his teams were 172-19. His 1966 team finished 2nd in the state. In 1970 he moved to Three Rivers Community College. In nine seasons as head coach his teams have won 228 games while losing only 79. His teams have appeared in the National Junior College Tournament on four occasions, winning 13 games and losing only 3. His team won the 1978-79 National Championship and he was named National "JUCO" Tournament "Coach of the Year."

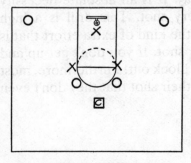

Diagram 79A

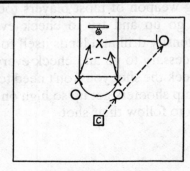

Diagram 79B

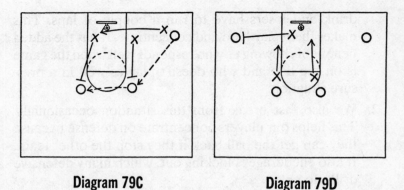

Diagram 79C   **Diagram 79D**

SHOT-CHECK DRILL: There is an overload situation involved here. Three defensive players must guard four offensive players. The coach starts with the ball and passes to one of the four offensive players to start the drill. The offensive players pass it around the horn and are ready to take a jump shot when they have it. There should be no skipping of passes in the beginning. As players get more adept you can allow this. The defensive players must drop to the line of the ball on passes to the corners (Diagram 79B). The back defensive man has the toughest job. The coach should never be quite satisfied with the effort exerted. The difference between checking a shot or not is a matter of inches. Total effort is necessary.

Special Value of the Drill: The jump shot is the primary scoring weapon of most players today. It is an absolute necessity to go up and try to check every shot. This drill is a high intensity drill and lends itself to the kind of extra effort that is necessary to go and check every shot. If you don't get up and check the shot you won't need to block out! Furthermore, most jump shooters get up so high on their shot that they don't even try to follow their shot.

RON NIKCEVICH
Lyons Township High School, La Grange, Illinois

Ron Nikcevich became the head basketball coach at River-side-Brookfield Township High School in Riverside, Illinois in 1961. During eight seasons his teams won two championships while compiling a record of 100-79. In 1969 he moved to Lyons Township High School in La Grange, Illinois. In ten years of coaching, his record now stands at 203 wins against only 57 losses. This includes 21 championships, among which was a perfect 31-0 season when his team was the Illinois State Champ.

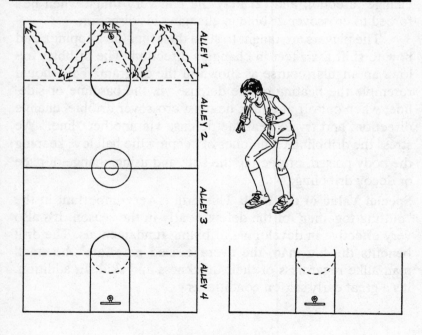

Diagram 80

TOWEL DRILL: Players pair up in four alleys according to the most desirable match-ups — by position, by speed and quickness, or perhaps a big, slow man paired with a quick little man. The defensive player assumes a stance with one leg slightly in advance of the other. The head should be the midway point between the spread of the legs and should act as a balance to prevent body weight from being overshifted too much on one leg. The defensive must begin and *remain* in a very low position throughout the drill. This is effeted by "tugging" towel, which is held across the back of the neck.

For the purpose of this drill we attempt to impart only two defensive principles which enable the defense to "beat" the offense: (1) Beat the dribbler to a line and force him to change direction and (2) Play the ball very tough when he's forced to crossover dribble in changing his direction.

The players are taught to slide their feet (no hopping), and how to shift their feet in changing direction. The dribbler follows an angular course as shown in the diagram. This should resemble the beating of the defense via the baseline or sideline; when cut off at a line, he must crossover dribble, change direction, and try to beat the defense via another "line." We stress the dribbling techniques of keeping the ball low, keeping the body poised, protecting the ball, and using change-of-pace or decoy dribbling.

Special Value of the Drill: This drill is very important in the "putting together" of the defense early in the season. It's also very effective in developing dribbling fundamentals. The drill benefits the big man, the average-sized man, and the small man alike regardless of their quickness and skill. In addition, it's a great early season conditioner.

DON REID
Merced College

Don Reid began his coaching career at Manteca High School, where he compiled a 106-29 won-loss record; then he moved to Merced College (California). During 16 seasons at Merced he has won 347 games while losing only 157. His teams have finished first or second in thirteen out of fifteen years of CCCCAA play. He was named the California J.C. (Division II) "Coach of the Year" in 1978 when his team won the State Championship. He was named as the Coach of the California Junior College All-Stars at the National AAU Tournament in Baton Rouge, Louisiana in 1975. The All-Star Team placed 2nd for their best ever finish.

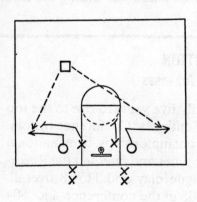

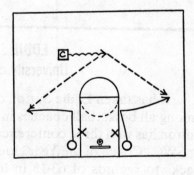

Diagram 81A   **Diagram 81B**

TWO-LINE BLOCK OUT DRILL: The ball starts with the coach who may pass to either forward as he breaks into position to receive the ball. The ballside defender works on fronting the cutter and the helpside defender attempts to stay one step off the line of the ball with one foot in the lane. When the ball is passed, the ballside defender guards the line and stops penetration. If the ball is thrown cross-court, the helpside defender closes out on the ball and the ballside defender gets to a help position. The coach may change sides on the dribble during the drill. The offensive players may shoot or drive if they are open. The coach ends up doing most of the shooting, and the primary purpose of the drill is to work on blocking off the defensive board from both the ballside and the helpside. The drill works better if the offensive player on the helpside plays wide most of the time.

Special Value of the Drill: The drill provides practice on several important skills. It sets up realistic court situations and it is easy for the coach to correct errors that occur during the drill.

EDDIE SUTTON
University of Arkansas

It has taken Eddie Sutton only five years to rise to the top among all basketball coaches in Southwest Conference history. Sutton has won three conference championships, been national or SWC "Coach of the Year" four times and directed the Razorbacks to records of 63-15 in league play and 115-28 overall. Those winning percentages of .808 in the conference and .804 for the season play are the two best records ever achieved in Southwest Conference history. In addition, Sutton is the only coach in SWC history to put together three consecutive seasons of 20 victories or more. Sutton's ten-year collegiate record is 201-77. He came to Arkansas from Creighton, where he enjoyed 82-50 success. His last team at Creighton was ranked 14th nationally and finished 23-6. Sutton played at Oklahoma State under coach Henry Iba. After serving a year as a graduate assistant to Iba, Sutton became head coach at Tulsa, Okla., Central High School, where his teams had a six-year record of 119-51. He began his collegiate coaching career at Southern Idaho, building an 83-14 record.

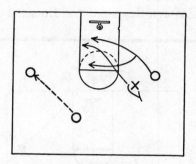

Diagram 82

WING-POST DENIAL DRILL: The defensive forward contests the guard to forward pass. The offensive guard then passes to the weakside forward. The offensive forward may flash to either a low post or high post position, and the defensive forward must deny him the ball at either position.

Special Value of the Drill: Included within the drill is perimeter defense one pass away, as well as the teaching of post defense when the player is flashed inside.

RICHARD SAUERS
State University of New York at Albany

Dr. Richard Sauers is currently in his 25th season at State University of New York at Albany. He has a winning percentage of .677, the seventh best among all Division III active coaches. His 386 career victories rank him fourth in Division III in that statistic. No coach ranks above him in BOTH categories. In his 24-year coaching term, he never has had a losing season. Sauers' teams have been in four NCAA post-season tournaments and were the 1978 ECAC Division II-III Upstate New York champions. In 1969 Albany finished third in the NCAA Small College regional. In the initial NCAA Division III Eastern Regional in 1975, Albany finished fourth. The Great Danes hosted the 1977 Eastern Regional and finished second.

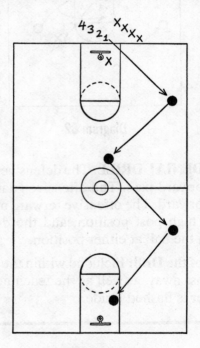

Diagram 83

ZIG-ZAG CHARGE DRILL: Player #1 tries to run in the direction indicated by the arrows toward the spots that are actually rubber discs on the floor. Player X must jump in the path of 1 and draw the charge in the desired manner. As soon as there is contact, both men get up and 1 runs toward the next disc in the zig-zag fashion indicated. X must get up and regain a position to take another charge. This goes on until 1 gets to the other end of the court. In all, four charges should be drawn. As soon as the first pair of players start toward the second disc, another pair of players start. When all pairs get to the end of the court, the players switch offense and defense and return.

Special Value of the Drill: The drill teaches *both* players to "take" contact. Mainly, however, it is a great way to teach a player the mechanics of drawing a charge.

GEORGE BIANCHI
Armstrong State College

George Bianchi's three year record at Armstrong State College is 54-29. His teams garnered the No. One Ranking in NCAA Division II basketball for 1978-79 and 1979-80. In three seasons his teams have been 12th, 2nd, and 1st in scoring. He was named NABC Division II South "Coach of the Year" in 1979.

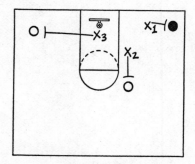

Diagram 84

3-ON-3 BLOCK OUT DRILL: X1 blocks out the shooter. One pass away, X2 moves to his man for a block out. X3 is in the help position three passes away, so he must *go and meet* his man for the block out outside the lane. The players rotate their positions after each shot unless the shot is made. One point is given for each rebound. If the offensive team gets the rebound and scores, give them one additional point. The drill ends when all players have rotated to all three positions both offensively and defensively. The group with the most points wins. The losers run a liner.

Part III

FAST BREAK DRILLS

GLEN KINNEY
Portland State University

Glen Kinney's coaching career began at Bend High School in Bend, Oregon in 1953. In eight years he recorded 112 wins against 56 losses and took four teams to the State Tournament. During his two seasons at South Bakersfield High School in California, he gave the school its first ever winning season. In 1963 he accepted the coaching reins at Corvallis (Oregon) High School. During twelve seasons his teams won nine championships and finished 2nd on three occasions. His 228-70 record included an undefeated 26-0 state championship. He moved to Central Oregon Community College in Bend, Oregon in 1975. In his three seasons there he compiled a 67-30 record while winning two State Championships. Kinney is now head basketball coach at Portland State University.

BLITZ DRILL: Seven X players and seven O players wear contrasting jerseys. In Diagram 85A three O's come up-court on a break vs. two X players back on defense. When the three O players *cross* centerline, X comes in from sideline as a defensive trailer, and O comes in from the other side as an offensive trailer. Limit the number of passes by the offense to insure fast break situation, and allow the offense only one follow shot. After the score, or defensive rebound, three players convert from defense to offense and start a break vs. two O players who have already set in tandem defense (Diagram 85B). The same rules apply as in Diagram 85A, so you end up with 4 on 3 break situation again. The drill continues, providing constant offense and defense break situations and constant running and ball handling vs. resistance. It may help to have someone chart the errors and keep score to provide extra incentive to excel in the drill.

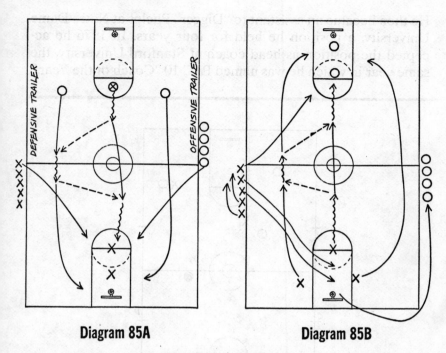

Diagram 85A   **Diagram 85B**

Special Value of the Drill: This drill has all the elements of the offensive and defensive breaking game. It is a good conditioning drill while handling the ball against pressure. If you wish, you can have the four offensive players convert to pressure defense and press the three break men till they get the ball over the center line.

DICK DiBIASO
Stanford University

Dick DiBiaso began his coaching career at Beacon (New York) High School. During six seasons as head coach his teams compiled 101 wins against only 16 losses. This included three league championships, two state section championships, and two undefeated seasons. In 1969 he moved to the University of Virginia and served for three seasons as an assistant coach.

He then became an assistant to "Digger" Phelps at Notre Dame University, a position he held for four years. In 1976 he accepted the position as head coach at Stanford University, the same year in which he was named PAC 10 "Coach of the Year."

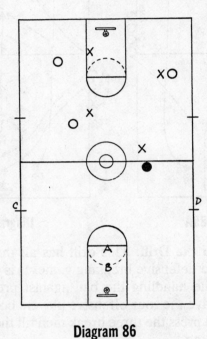

Diagram 86

FAST BREAK COMBINATION DRILL — 4-ON-4 OFFENSE VS. DEFENSE: The *Offense* must dribble across mid-court. The forwards must get open on their own. The offense is restricted to one dribble after the entry pass by the guard. The *Defense* uses the fast break after possession. A and B defend against the fast break. C and D enter the drill *after the ball passes them.* The drill ends on a score, turnover or possession by A and B team. A-B-C-D go on offense. The "O" team goes to defense. The "X" team stays to defend break.

Special Value of the Drill: The drill teaches initiation for guards and getting open for the forwards. It presents the different defensive situations and teaches passing, screening and movement for the offense.

DOM PERNO
University of Connecticut

Dom Perno's coaching career began at South Catholic High School in Hartford, Conn. In two seasons his teams recorded 31 wins against only 4 losses. From there he moved to St. Paul Catholic High School in Bristol, Conn. His 104-33 record over six years includes six appearances in the CIAC Tournament. In 1972 he became an assistant at the University of Connecticut, a position he held for five years before becoming the head coach in 1977. In his two seasons at the helm his teams have compiled a 32-23 record and won an ECAC New England Championship.

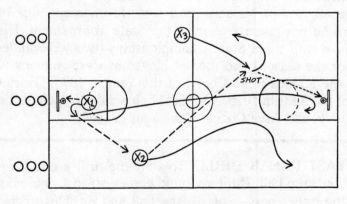

Diagram 87

FAST BREAK SETUP WITH TRANSITION: X1 is the rebounder, X2 is the outlet pass man and feeder, and X3 is the best shooter. This drill teaches many things: (1) rebounding, (2) accurate outlet passes, (3) feeding the shooter, (4) shooting the 12 foot jump shot at the end of the break, (5) rebounder transition to obtain rebound after the jump shot, and (6) moving quickly up and down the court with teammates. It is a 3 on 0 situation. X1 must hustle down-court to take the ball out of the basket or off the boards and start the break in the other direction. The ball should never touch the floor after the shot. The players return, fulfilling the same assignments.

JOHN LOCKE
Natoma High School, Natoma, Kansas

John Locke's remarkable coaching career spans a period of nearly 50 years! He spent 10 years at Conert High School, 10 years at Stockton High School, and 25 years at Natoma High School, all in Kansas, en route to his amazing overall record of 731 wins and only 213 losses. He, himself, played in the State Tournament in 1926, and then had the unique experience of coaching all five of his sons in a state tournament. On 14 occasions he has taken a team to the State Tournament. His teams have won three State Championships (two were undefeated for the season) and four of his teams were runnersup. He was the Kansas State Coach of the Year in 1975, District Coach of the Year in 1976, National High School Coach of the Year in 1976, and Area Coach of the Year in 1979.

5-MAN FAST BREAK DRILL: To start the drill a coach or player shoots the ball. If the rebound comes off to 1, 5 breaks out for the outlet pass, receives the ball and dribbles to the middle, never penetrating deeper than the free throw line at the opposite end of the court unless he goes all the way for the layup. If 5 picks the ball up outside the free throw line, he can shoot the jumper or pass off to 2 or 4 who have filled the out-

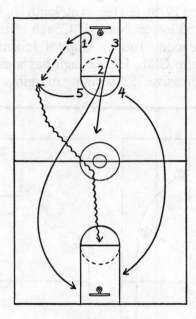

Diagram 88

side lanes. In the diagrammed situation 3 would be a trailer and 1 the safety coming up slowly as the play develops. The ball is passed out to the side the rebound comes off. If it comes off straight in front, the outlet pass is optional. Insist on all five players rebounding. If 4 or 5 gets the ball, he takes it down the middle lane. It is a race to see who can fill the outside lanes.

BILL HIMEBAUGH
South High School, Wichita, Kansas

Bill Himebaugh has been head basketball coach at Wichita South High School for eight seasons. During that time his team won a city championship, four invitational tournament championships, five sub-state championships, and two state championships (1977 and 1978). His teams at South High have recorded 123 wins against 53 losses. Named "Coach of the Year" by the Wichita Eagle-Beacon, Topeka Capitol Journal and Wichita Downtown Athletic Club, Himebaugh has a career record of 240-75 for an impressive 75% winning margin.

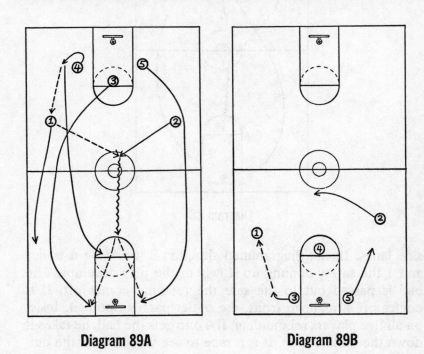

| Diagram 89A | Diagram 89B |

5-MAN WEAVE: This drill is a good fast break and conditioning drill. It has the outlet pass to your outside people, ball handling, plus the conditioning factor of running the full length of the court 6 to 8 times. The theory behind this drill is that you always have three men rebounding and you always have two for the outlet pass. The first three down the court are your rebounders and the last two go the outlet pass area.

Special Value of the Drill: This is primarily a fast break drill. I like it because everyone is involved in doing exactly what he will be doing in a game. It includes a lot of fundamentals such as defensive positioning to start the drill, rebounding, outlet passes, dribble, feed pass and shooting. The running involved is an aid in conditioning.

C.M. NEWTON
Vanderbilt University

Presently head coach at Vanderbilt, C.M. Newton has coached at Transylvania (Ky.) College. In 12 seasons he had a 169-137 record there. His 1963 team won an NAIA District championship and had a 20-8 record. In 1968 he began the major rebuilding project at the University of Alabama. By his fifth year, Alabama was in the semi-finals of the NIT and had a 22-8 record. That marked the first post-season national tournament for an Alabama basketball team. The Tide reeled off three consecutive SEC championships from 1974 to 1976 and in 1977, it was back again to the NIT semi-finals. A 25-6 record that year set a school record for most wins in a season. In addition to three NIT appearances, Newton took Alabama to two NCAA post-season tournaments. Under Newton's direction, Alabama won 22 or more games in six of his last seven seasons. He has been selected SEC "Coach of the Year" four times and has also been named the NCAA District III "Coach of the Year."

4-MAN BREAK: Put 4 men on the court as diagrammed. The coach shoots the ball. The guards watch the ball and go to outlet positions (the guard on the side the ball is rebounded goes to the outlet position at the foul line extended, and the other guard goes to the middle). This gives the rebounder two men close to him for a quick outlet pass. Middle men must react to the ball. The inside men rebound aggressively and make the outlet pass to either outlet man. Inside men then fill the open lane. Whichever inside man can get to the lane first, then the last man out becomes the trailer. Upon receipt of the outlet pass, the ball is taken to the middle quickly and a 3-line break with a trailer is established. From this break the layup or the good percentage jump shot can be taken. The trailer is an important addition because he can go to the open area late for the jump shot.

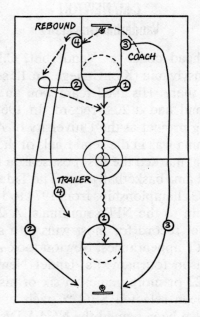

Diagram 90

Special Value of the Drill: This drill is the central drill in teaching the fast break. It stresses (1) the outlet position and outlet pass, (2) filling the lanes, and (4) the trailer or 4th man out in the break. We run this 10 to 15 minutes every day and it is not only good in teaching the fast break but is an excellent drill in conditioning.

JAMES DUTCHER
University of Minnesota

James Dutcher's coaching career began at Alpena High School. The next year he became the Head Basketball Coach and Athletic Director at Alpena Community College in Michigan. He recorded 105 wins against 70 losses, was twice named conference "Coach of the Year," and appeared at the National Junior College Tournament. In 1966 he moved to Eastern Michigan University where he was twice named NAIA District "Coach of the Year." In six seasons his record was 126-50, and his teams appeared in the national tournament on five occasions. During the next three seasons, while he served as an assistant at the University of Michigan, the team's record was 55-26 and they appeared in two NCAA regionals. In 1975 he became the head coach at the University of Minnesota. At Minnesota his teams have qualified for the NCAA Tournament in 1976 and 1977, and reached the NIT finals in 1980.

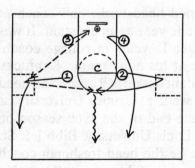

Diagram 91A

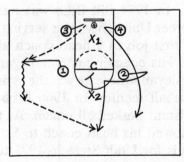

Diagram 91B

4-MAN BREAK DRILL: 1 and 2 take the guard positions, 3 and 4 take the forward positions, and the coach shoots. If 3 rebounds, he immediately hits 1 who has slid to the outlet square, 2 comes directly toward 1 for the second pass, and 4 sprints to the outside wing. The three-lane break is taken to the other end, with 3 becoming the trailer. Upon reaching the other end, 1 and 2 take the forward positions, 3 and 4 take the guard positions, and they repeat the drill coming back. This gives all the players the opportunity to handle the various spots. To closer approximate game conditions, we now add two defensive men, as shown in Diagram 91B. X1 harasses the rebounder to make the outlet pass more difficult while X2 tries to steal either the outlet pass or the second pass to the middle. If X2 covers the outlet man, the latter releases down court immediately. If X2 plays to intercept the second pass, the outlet man dribbles down his wing and passes to the middle at the first opportunity. This drill forces us to adjust to the defense.

BILL BIBB
Mercer University

In 1974 Bill Bibb was named head basketball coach at Mercer University after serving one year as an assistant. It was his first job as a head coach after 15 years in college coaching. His coaching career began at his alma mater, Kentucky Wesleyan, where he was the assistant basketball coach and head baseball mentor. In 1966 Bibb went to Trinity University as assistant basketball coach. At the end of the 1969 season he followed his head coach to St. Louis University. Bibb left St. Louis for Utah State in 1971 to be the head freshman coach and assistant varsity coach. He came to Mercer in the spring of 1973 as assistant basketball coach. In 1981 Mercer made its first appearance in an NCAA Tournament.

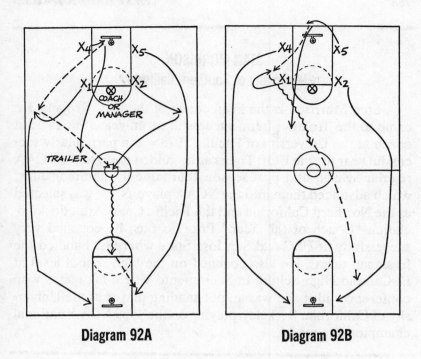

Diagram 92A   **Diagram 92B**

4-MAN FAST BREAK DRILL: This may be run from a re-bounded shot or from a missed free throw situation. The coach or manager shoots the ball from the free throw line. X4 and X5 are the rebounders. In the diagram, X4 rebounds the ball and throws out to X1 on his side and then becomes a trailer. X5 leaves to fill the lane as soon as he sees X4's rebound. X2 moves to the side for an outlet pass. If it goes to the opposite side he moves to the middle for a pass and leads the break. X1 receives the outlet and passes to X2 to get the ball in the middle, then he fills the lane. If X1 is covered in the middle, X2 can dribble into the middle and X1 can fill his outside lane. If the free throw is made, the opposite guard hooks back into the middle to receive the inbounds pass and then he brings it up the middle on a dribble as the other players fill the lanes.

STAN MORRISON
University of Southern California

Stan Morrison is the head coach of the USC Trojans. He came to the Trojans after a successful seven-year stint as head coach at the University of Pacific. 1978 was a particularly successful year for the UOP Tigers as he guided them to the PCAA regular season and post-season tournament championships, which advanced them into the NCAA playoffs. He was selected as the Northern California and the Pacific Coast Athletic Association "Coach of the Year." Prior to this, he coached very successfully at USC and San Jose State where he handled the freshman teams. He also coached on the high school level at El Camino High School in Sacramento where his teams won conference titles. He was an outstanding player at the University of California, Berkeley, playing on the 1959 NCAA national championship team.

4-ON-2 PLUS 2 DRILL: The drill begins with four offensive and four defensive players (Diagram 93A). The ball is shot by one of the guards and rebounded by one of the big players. We start the offensive rebounding at least 15 feet from the basket to insure difficulty in the rebounding block-off technique employed by our big people. Once the rebound is secure, the offensive rebounders are not to interfere with this outlet pass or the fast break. The two guards can do whatever they want to stop the fast break, thus creating the need for both verbal and visual communication among the fast breaking players.

The big man who doesn't get the rebound must "pull opposite" to get the third lane filled for the fast break. The rebounder is our "trailer" and runs to a pre-determined spot.

The conclusion of the fast break is when the defensive guards get control of the ball either through a made basket, a rebound, or an interception. The ball must then be taken out of

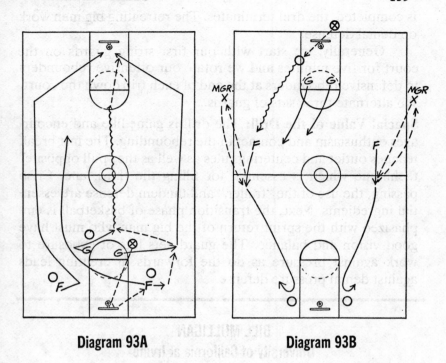

Diagram 93A   **Diagram 93B**

bounds (Diagram 93B). The first pass inbound is permitted without pressure. Once the ball is inbounded, the guards are in a full court man-to-man "force sideline" defensive situation. Good communication verbally between the guards is necessary. The instant the fast break terminates, the big men must turn and sprint in a straight line with their backs to the nearest sideline and their heads over their shoulders looking back at the ball.

Managers will be standing at each free throw line extended and instructed to throw the ball as hard as they can at the head of the retreating big man. With good vision, he will see the ball (which is not thrown until he reaches the half-court line) and he is to catch it, come to a two foot stop without traveling or using a dribble. He then is to toss the ball to the manager and continue sprinting down to find the two offensive rebounders to create leads to receive an entry pass. Once the pass is completed, the drill terminates. The retreating big men work on denial defense.

Generally, we start with our first string guards on the court for five minutes and we rotate our offensive rebounders to defensive rebounders at the end of each trip down the court. We alternate three sets of guards.

Special Value of the Drill: The drill is game-like and encourages enthusiasm and contact in the rebounding. The fast break teaches outlet and centering rules as well as the "pull opposite" technique which is essential for filling the third lane. Crisp passing, the use of the "trailer," and tandem defense are essential ingredients. Next, the transition phase of basketball is emphasized with the sprint return of the big man who must have good vision and balance. The guard gets lots of exposure to work against pressure as do the forwards in creating leads against denial pressure defense.

BILL MULLIGAN
University of California at Irvine

With 24 years of basketball coaching experience behind him, Bill Mulligan made his debut as a major college head coach in 1980 at UC Irvine. In 14 years of head coaching at the Community College level (9 at Riverside Community College and 5 at Saddleback Community College) he has compiled an impressive record of 332-118. In his least successful season, his team won 18 games and he has never had a losing season. In 1979 he led the Gauchos of Saddleback College to a 34-1 record, their fourth conference title, and the semifinals of the state tournament. Mulligan's teams have led the state in scoring in each of the last three seasons by averaging 107, 97, and 108 points. He also coached on the high school level at Long Beach Poly. Over four seasons he coached them to two CIF championships, second in the CIF once, and fourth in the CIG on another occasion.

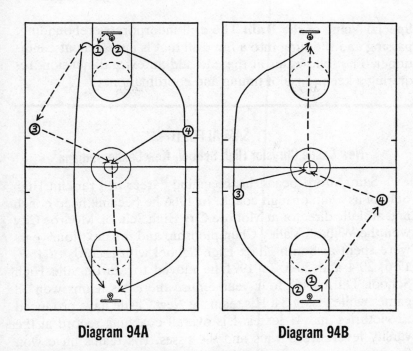

Diagram 94A   **Diagram 94B**

REBOUND, OUTLET, AND GO DRILL: Two players take positions in the lane and two are stationed at the hash marks. The drill starts with 2 tossing the ball over the basket and off the glass for 1 to rebound. As soon as he tosses the ball, 2 breaks out on a dead sprint to the outside break lane. When he reaches the free throw line extended at the other end of the court he cuts to the basket looking for a pass. 1 rebounds and outlets to 3 and then sprints to the other end to rebound the shot. 3 receives the pass at the hash mark and passes it to 4 breaking to the middle. After 4 receives the pass he makes a long lead pass *from mid-court* to 2 going in for the layup. 4 and 3 go to the hash marks at the other half of the court to repeat the sequence. 2 lays the ball in and then sprints to the other basket. 1 rebounds and outlets to 4 who in turn passes to 3 at mid-court. The drill concludes with 2 laying the ball on the glass, 3 following the "shot" and tipping it up on the glass, 4 following the tip with one of his own, and a slam by 1 (if possible).

Special Value of the Drill: The drill incorporates rebounding, passing and shooting into a fun drill that is an excellent conditioner. The follow tips at the end add an extra dimension, requiring a keen sense of timing and coordination.

SAM ALFORD
New Castle Chrysler High School, New Castle, Indiana

Sam Alford began his coaching career at Franklin High School as a junior high coach. In 1966 he became head coach and athletic director at Monroe City High School. Monroe City won the Wabash Valley Championship and the next four years were spent at South Knox High School with records of 15-7, 17-6, 20-4 and 20-3. In 1971 he moved to Martinsville High School. During his four year tenure there his teams won 58 games while losing 34. His teams at New Castle have produced 52 victories and 41 losses. His overall coaching record at the varsity level is 203 wins and 99 losses. His teams have won five conference titles, five holiday tournaments and five sectionals. He was voted Indiana District "Coach of the Year" in 1979, making him the first coach in Indiana to receive the award in two different districts.

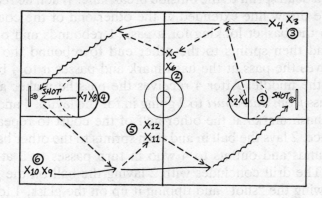

Diagram 95

6-LINE LAYUP DRILL: X1 hits X4 with an outlet pass. X4 hits X5 with a sharp, quick pass. X5 returns a lead pass to X4 and X4 drives in for the layup. On the other side of the floor with a second ball, X7 hits X9 with an outlet pass. X9 then passes to X11. X11 returns a lead pass to X9 and X9 drives in for the layup. The circled numbers in the diagram indicate the movement of the players after completing each assignment.

Special Value of the Drill: The drill combines passing, dribbling, and shooting with constant movement. It provides practice in fast break ball handling and it can easily replace the old half-court layup drill.

KEN TRICKEY
Oklahoma City University

Ken Trickey's collegiate coaching career began as an assistant basketball coach and head baseball coach at Middle Tennessee. In 1965 he became the head basketball coach. In 1969 he moved to Oral Roberts University and spent five years building them into a national power leading the Titans to two NITs and one National Collegiate playoff. He won 21 or more games each year there. His teams were noted for their high scoring. His 1971 team established a NCAA record by averaging 105.1 points per game, and his 1972-73 team also led the nation in scoring. Trickey's teams played in the 1972 and 1973 NIT Classics, and in 1974 his team was runnerup in the Midwest NCAA Regional. His overall college record now stands at 231-135.

3-MAN FAST BREAK DRILL: The middle man 1 stops at the free throw line. The shooter 2 keeps running to fill the lane. Non-shooter 3 rebounds and passes to middle man 1 who has released to the wing. Middle man 1 returns the ball to the non-shooter 3 who becomes the middle man on the return trip.

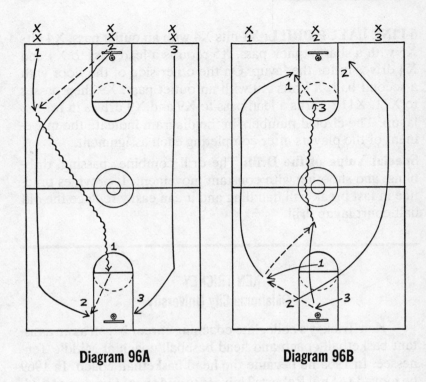

Diagram 96A   **Diagram 96B**

Note: If middle man 1 shoots, he will still break to the wing for the outlet pass. The non-rebounder will fill the opposite lane. The rebounder will make the outlet pass and fill the middle for a return pass.

This drill gives you all options in running the fast break. We use chairs at the free throw line extended and underneath the basket to make the cutters run their routes. We create pressure at the middle of the floor so the middle man with the ball has to recognize defenses. The drill: (1) gives us a good outlet pass; (2) makes us fill lanes properly; (3) ball stops at the free throw line for a short jump shot; (4) guards pass to cutters for layup shots; (5) cutters cross under for a delayed short jump shot; (6) cutters stop just inside free throw line for a short jump shot off the board; (7) it also is a superb conditioning drill. By adding chairs at the free throw line extended, players must run 94 feet. You can use two balls in the drill. When the first group is laying the ball on the glass on their return up the floor, the second group starts. At OCU we run this drill 15 minutes every day.

FRANK CRISAFI
East Haven High School, East Haven, Connecticut

Frank Crisafi has been the Head Basketball Coach at East Haven High School in East Haven, Connecticut for 32 years. During this time he has compiled an amazing 500 wins against only 195 losses for a winning percentage of .719. His teams have been Housatonic League champions eleven times. On five occasions his teams have won the State of Connecticut championship, and he has claimed one New England Championship. During one point in his career his teams recorded 77 straight wins.

3-MAN FIGURE 8 FAST BREAK DRILL: O1 passes to O2 and cuts behind. O2 passes to O3 who is coming to the middle. O3 passes to cutting O1 for a layup. Only three passes are allowed at the beginning with no dribbling. Later, as many passes as the coach likes may be allowed depending on the skill of the personnel and the coach's demands. To really put pressure on the players, a time limit averaging five seconds per trip may be imposed.

Special Value of the Drill: It is a real conditioner. It improves ball handling and passing on the move. It causes the players to talk and communicate while being an excellent morale builder.

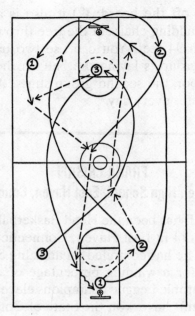

Diagram 97

DAN BELLUOMINI
University of San Francisco

In the early sixties Dan Belluomini played in USF's back-court on three WCAC championship teams. After graduation from USF in 1964, he went back to coach at his alma mater, St. Ignatius High School in San Francisco for two years before moving to Willow Glen High School in San Jose. He guided that squad to a league championship and two second place finishes. After six seasons as an assistant coach at USF, he took over the helm of the Dons as head coach for the 1978-79 season. In his first year his team recorded 23 wins against 7 losses and Coach Belluomini was named WCAC and District XIV "Coach of the Year."

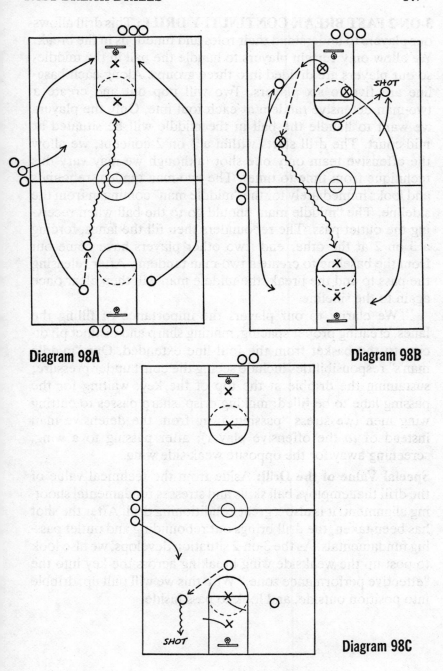

Diagram 98A

Diagram 98B

Diagram 98C

3-ON-2 FAST BREAK CONTINUITY DRILL: This drill allows our players to understand their roles and functions in the break. We allow only certain players to handle the ball in the middle, so our players are divided into three groups. Along each baseline are five to six players. Two will pop out and create a two-man defensive tandem at each foul line. Only the players we want to handle the ball in the middle will be situated at mid-court. The drill starts within a 3 on 2 concept; we allow the offensive team only one shot (although we may vary this technique from time to time). The two-man tandem rebounds and looks immediately for the "middle man" coming in from the sideline. The "middle man" should go to the ball when receiving the outlet pass. The rebounders then fill the lanes, forcing a 3 on 2 at the other end (two other players have come out from the baseline to create a two-man tandem). After releasing the pass to end the break, the middle man will then clear once again to the sideline.

We clarify to our players the importance of filling the lanes, creating proper spacing, making sharp and distinct pivot-cuts to the basket from the foul line extended. Our "middle man's" responsibilities include seeing the court under pressure; sustaining the dribble at the top of the key; waiting for the passing lane to be filled; making crisp, sharp passes to cutting wing men (we stress "passing *away* from the defensive man instead of *to* the offensive player); after passing to a wing, screening away for the opposite weak-side wing.

Special Value of the Drill: Aside from the technical value of the drill that employs ball skills and stresses fundamental shooting alignment, it is also a great conditioning drill. After the shot has been taken, the drill brings out rebounding and outlet passing fundamentals. As the 3-on-2 situation develops, we also look to post up the weakside wing breaking across the key into the "effective performance zone." With this we will pull up, dribble into position outside, and look to pass inside.

HAL NUNNALLY
Randolph-Macon College

Hal Nunnally spent eight seasons as the basketball coach at Tidewater Academy in Virginia. His 169-71 record included the distinction as Outstanding Private School Basketball Team in Virginia during the 1971-72 season. In 1973 he became the freshmen basketball coach at Randolph-Macon College. After three seasons he was named head coach. In his five year tenure as head coach his teams have recorded 80 wins against 55 losses. In 1977 they were NCAA Division II finalists, and he was a "Coach of the Year" nominee.

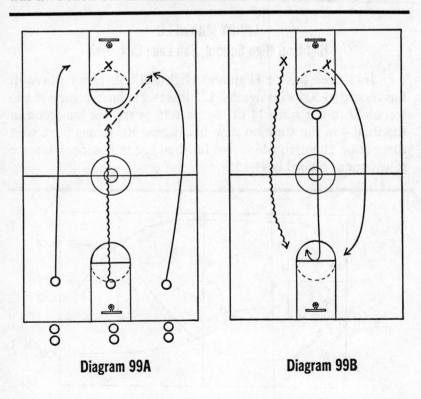

Diagram 99A   **Diagram 99B**

3-ON-2 TO 2-ON-1 FAST BREAK DRILL: Three offensive men attack two defensive men in primary fast break situation. The offense is allowed two passes after the ball goes to either wing. On missed shots the offense is allowed only a power move off the rebound for a score. On made shots the offensive wing must make the inbounds pass for the two defensive players. After made or missed shots, the offensive point man becomes the defensive player in a 2-on-1 situation. The two original defensive players rebound or take the inbounds pass and attack 2 on 1, moving to the opposite end of the court. The drill is continuous and all players move through all lines.

LARRY MAXWELL
Highland High School, Salt Lake City, Utah

In 19 seasons at Highland High School, Larry Maxwell has recorded 304 wins against 132 losses. He has finished in the top eight in the state 14 of the past 16 years. He has been in the final 4 in the state on nine occasions. His teams have won three state championships and finished second twice. His state tournament record is 41-15.

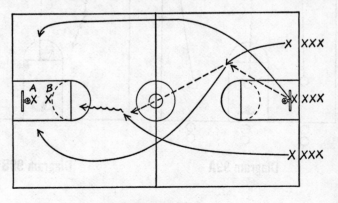

Diagram 100

3-2 DRILL: In this drill we have 3 on 2 going down (in a semi figure-8 weave) and a 2 on 1 coming back. The player of the three on offense who shoots hustles back and becomes the defense for the 2 on 1 coming back. A and B (who were the defense for the 3 on 2) become the offense for the 2 on 1. The 2 offensive players who didn't shoot on the 3 on 2 become the defense for the next group and then become the offense for the 2 on 1. The drill can be changed to accommodate any number combinations (as long as you bring back the same number you send down).

ROLLAND TODD
Santa Ana College

After an outstanding career as a player at the collegiate and professional level, Rolland Todd entered the coaching profession. In rapid succession he went from high school coaching (Ranier Beach High, Wash.) to college assistant (Riverside C.C. & Cal State L.A.) to the head coach's job at the University of Nevada at Las Vegas. There he built the school's basketball program into a major college power, posting a 96-40 record. In 1970 he was hired as the first coach of the Portland Trail Blazers, a job he held for two years. As the head coach at Santa Ana College, his teams have won two South Coast Conference Championships, been runnerup once, and sport an overall 68-25 record.

2-MAN FAST BREAK DRILL: The rebounder tosses the ball off the backboard and rebounds it. Insist that a proper turn and outlet pass be made to start the break. The outlet man starts inside the free throw area and then breaks to the outlet spot (we use the hash mark as our guide) calling "Outlet," so the rebounder can locate him by sound. The rebounder fills the lane by running *directly* from the rebound spot to the

intersection of half court line and out of bounds. At the hash
mark in the offensive end of the court he makes a 45° cut to
the basket. The outlet man has put the ball on the floor to the
middle of the court. His goal is to hit the wing just after he
makes the 45° cut. He continues on to the free throw line,
pauses as the ball is laid up, then busts for the rebound. Going
back the other way, the wing is sprinting to half court, the
rebounder puts the ball on the floor (simulating a guard rebound in a game) looking for a pass to the wing as soon as
possible after the wing crosses mid-court. After the pass he will
again sprint to the free throw line at the other end. For variety
you can have the wings pull up for a jumper or hit the man
at the free throw line for a jumper.

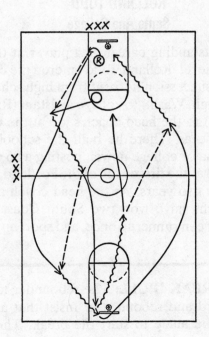

Diagram 101

Special Value of the Drill: This drill includes the basic elements of the break. It allows us to concentrate on proper lane responsibilities. It gives our outlet people a chance to develop a proper sense of timing on their passes without a whole lot of confusion. Also, it is a great conditioner.

NICK MACARCHUK
Canisius College

In nine seasons at St. Thomas More Prep School, Nick Macarchuk built an impressive 142-50 record which included three New England Championships. In 1972 he accepted the position as Head Basketball Coach at Providence College. During five seasons he compiled 119 wins against only 36 losses and made an appearance in the NCAA "final four." In 1977 he moved to Canisius College.

2-1-2 DRILL: We call this our 2-1-2 Drill and use it every day. Because we use the running game, this is an excellent practice drill for the break and is also very good for conditioning. The three X's make it difficult to inlet the ball from 5 to 1. They can double team 1 and/or pressure 5 and 4. Once the ball is inbounded, only the three X's in the backcourt can defend. Once the ball crosses the 10 second line, now only the two X's in the front court can play defense. The middle X is a rover and is free to do what he likes on defense. The drill is continuous and ends when the offense has gone up and down the court and scored ten baskets *or* the defense has made three points (misses shot and rebound or caused a turnover). The 5 man must take the ball out after each made field goal and inlet it to the 1 man; the 2 man always sprints the right lane; the 3 man sprints the left lane; 4 and 5 trail.

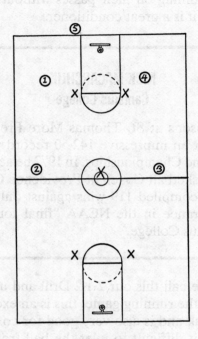

Diagram 102

Part IV

COMBINATION DRILLS

JOEDY GARDNER
Northern Arizona University

Joedy Gardner played collegiate basketball at West Virginia University with such well known teammates as Hot Rod Hundley and Jerry West. He captained the 1958 Mountaineer team that finished 26-2 and was ranked Number 1. After college, Gardner spent 10 years in the Marine Corps and attained the rank of major. He was a jet pilot with over 1000 missions in Vietnam. In 1972 he began his career as a head coach by taking over the reins at Arizona Western Junior College. He was selected as Arizona "Coah of the Year" in 1973. Coach Gardner's overall head coaching record is 136-91. In his first season in the Big Sky Conference he was named Big Sky "Coach of the Year."

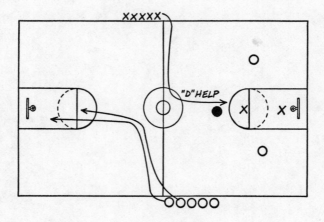

Diagram 103

ATTACK DRILL: This drill uses a minimum of 12 players. It is a 2 on 3 that becomes a 3 on 3 after the ball passes the midcourt plane. All players must enter the floor from the mid-

156

court out of bounds point. They must run up the line and place one foot inside the center circle before proceeding to a defensive help position and the offensive end of the court. Many rules may be placed into the drill. Here are a few examples:

1. No dribbling — or only certain players may dribble.
2. Middle man on offense cannot enter 3 second lane or it counts as a turnover.
3. Call all fouls; call only certain fouls.
4. Keep defensive players in mid-court circle until the "other" team on the offensive end gains possession of the ball.
5. Allow only certain types of shots to count.
6. Allow only certain players to score.
7. Make all players dribble three times before shooting.
8. Keep the defense on the floor until the mid-court line coming back (this simulates full court pressure).

Any rule imaginable can be used to control the type of play the coach desires. The game can be played like a real game. The team scoring or losing then must run off the court and proceed to the end of their respective team line.

Special Value of the Drill: It is a fast break/conditioning drill that can be controlled to emphasize any fundamental desired. It is a fun drill that is very competitive. Most players think of it as an offensive game, but great emphasis can be placed on *defense* or passing or dribbling or non-dribbling, etc.

JAMES HASTINGS
Central High School, Duluth, Minnesota

In 28 seasons as a head basketball coach, James Hastings has compiled a record of 447 wins against only 160 losses. This includes ten conference championships, three 2nd place finishes in the state tournament, and three state championships. His state tournament record stands at 18-4. He has won seven

"Coach of the Year" awards and was the 1979 National High School Athletic Coaches Association Region Six "Coach of the Year" and National Runner-up.

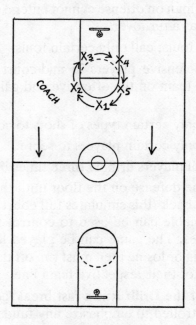

Diagram 104

CIRCLE DRILL: Place five players on the perimeter of the free throw circle, properly spaced. The coach stands off to the side with a ball. The coach starts the drill with a verbal command, "Circle right (or left)." The players graduate from half speed to full speed as they become accustomed to the fundamentals of the drill. When the coach feels they're in the proper circle rhythm, he shouts, "Reverse left" — they are to use the proper pivot technique — or "Reverse right."

To add the element of calisthenics to the drill: "Circle right" — "Reverse left" — "On your backs, in count unison, 5 sit ups" — "Up" — "Circle right" — "On your chests, in count unison, 10 push ups" — etc. (The coach can change the rhythm any way he desires.) To break the drill, simply call, "Ball."

Use any of these options: (1) throw the ball off the boards, (2) throw the ball into the pack, or (3) throw the ball anywhere in the gym. The players are to gain possession then fast break to the opposite basket. The next five players move into the circle and the drill begins again. When one group is occupying the circle, the other groups are executing any number of ball handling and passing drills.

Special Value of the Drill: It is a super conditioner. The players must listen and concentrate. It creates good discipline. The players put pressure on one another to execute it properly, thus developing responsibility.

LEE ROSE
University of South Florida

Lee Rose's coaching career began at Transylvania University. In 1964 he became the head coach. His teams won 160 games while losing 57, appeared in six Division II Regional Tournaments, and was an NAIA Finalist. He moved to the University of North Carolina at Charlotte and his teams won 72 while losing only 18. In each of his three years his teams were conference champions. Included in this was an NIT Runner-up and 4th in the NCAA Final Four. He became the head coach at Purdue in 1978, and in 1979-80 his team was 3rd in the NCAA Final Four. His overall record is 282-93 for a winning percentage of .752, giving him the third best winning percentage of active major college basketball coaches. In 1980 he became head coach at the University of South Florida, and he led them to the NIT in his first season.

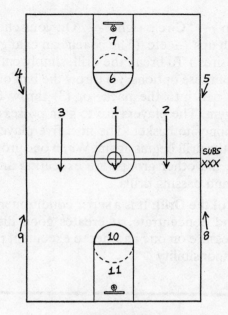

Diagram 105

11-MAN DRILL: We teach the point man on defense to stop the ball at the top of the circle and the bottom man to cover the first pass. After the first pass, the point defensive player drops back to cover the basket. Offensive players must take advantage of the 3-on-2 situation after the basketball is rebounded. After a missed shot or a made field goal, the rebounder outlets to one of the stationary wing players. After the outlet, the rebounder follows his pass, and we are back into a 3-on-2 going the other way. When a mistake is made, we replace the person responsible for the mistake with one of the substitutes who are placed at the mid-court line, this giving us continual movement.

Special Value of the Drill: We like the 11 man drill because it gives our players work on shooting, passing, dribbling, rebounding (boxing out), two and three man defenses, and offensive play. We also find that it is fun for our players as well as being a good conditioning drill.

DICK BERNING
St. Xavier High School, Cincinnati, Ohio

A 1953 graduate of Xavier University, Dick Berning began his coaching career the next year at St. Xavier High School in Cincinnati, Ohio. His teams have won 343 games while losing only 166. During this 24-year stretch he has won nine league championships, four district titles, and one regional championship. In 1965 his team was the State Runner-up in the AAA Division.

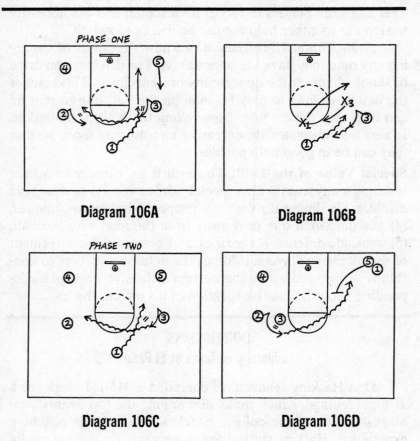

Diagram 106A

Diagram 106B

Diagram 106C

Diagram 106D

5-MAN WEAVE: Players rotate clockwise each time a new sequence is started.

Phase One: The Offensive team runs a five man weave (initially do not let them go too fast). There is to be no screening nor attempts to take the ball to the basket on a dribble. This teaches players how to slide through. We teach players one rule to cover all situations. "As you slide through, there is always one player between you and the man you are guarding. Never be the fourth man."

Phase Two: The offensive man starting in the corner will get a screen for the dribbler instead of continuing the weave. This helps the players to recognize a screen and the necessity to step out to either help out on the ball or to switch.

Phase Three: The offensive men have the option of screening any time they have the opportunity. The dribbler can drive or shoot whenever the opportunity presents itself. This teaches the defensive man to play his man on the ball side so that he can help stop the dribbler from taking the ball to the basket. It also teaches weakside defensive men to play loose so that they can be in good help position.

Special Value of the Drill: The drill is an excellent tool for teaching many team skills, especially defensive: (1) guarding the dribbler, (2) sliding through, (3) proper switching techniques, (4) guarding man one pass away from the man with the ball, (5) weakside defense, (6) boxing out. Because of the movement of the offensive players, it forces the defensive players to constantly adjust and apply the correct defensive principles, depending upon the relative location of his man to the ball.

DON HASKINS
University of Texas at El Paso

Don Haskins' teams have compiled a 315-151 mark for a .676 percentage, which ranks him among the top twenty winningest active major college coaches. Prior to his coaching experience, Haskins starred for three years on the nationally ranked team coached by Henry Iba. His first coaching venture came at Benjamin, Texas. Nex year he moved to Hedley, Texas, where he posted a record of 115-26. Next it was Dumas, Texas, where he compiled 25-wins against 7 losses and a trip to the state tournament. He then accepted the head coaching job at UTEP in 1961. In 1972 he was selected as an assistant coach for the U.S. Olympic Team participating in the Summer Games in Munich, Germany. He has taken eight teams to post-season tournaments, and in 1966 his team won the NCAA Championship.

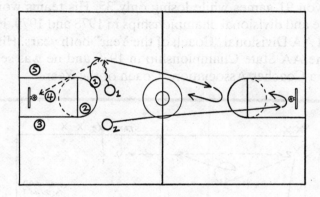

Diagram 107

5-ON-2 TRANSITION DRILL: The object of the drill is to teach our players to stop penetration of the basketball to a good shooting position with five offensive players on the floor. O1 and O2 play a 2-on-2 game against D1 and D2. D3, D4 and D5 move as if covering invisible men, but do not interfere with the 2-on-2 game. When O1 shoots the ball, D3, D4 and D5 immediately block out and rebound. O1 and O2 become defensive players. Because O2 is not involved in shooting the ball, he will probably be back first. He *sprints* to the defensive basket. O1 *sprints* to our defensive end of the floor and works himself back to the ten-second line. O2 works his way toward the ten-second line to about the top of the key (only after O1 has the

ten-second secure). These two defensive men are attacked by
the five players who are now on offense. After the ball is lost
or the basket is made, the 1 and 2 men on both teams switch
sides and the drill is run in the other direction.

JACK RENKENS
Winslow High School, Winslow, Arizona

Jack Renkens has been the head coach of the Winslow
Bulldogs for the past five years. During this time his teams
have won 91 games while losing only 35. His teams won conference and divisional championships in 1978 and 1979. He was
named AA Divisional "Coach of the Year" both years. His team
won the AA State Championship in 1979 and he was selected
Arizona Coaches Association "Coach of the Year."

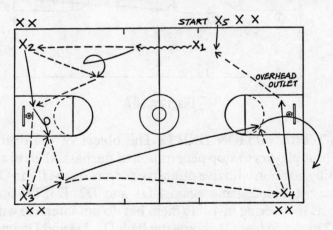

Diagram 108

4-CORNER PASS DRILL: This 4-corner pass drill combines
four different passes, a pivot and a lay-in. The drill starts at the
hash mark with two balls. The first man dribbles past mid-court
and throws a chest pass to the man in the corner (X2). He

receives a return pass, jump stops, pivots, and returns the ball to the corner man who is now breaking for the next corner. After X2 receives the pass he throws a bounce pass to X3, receives a return pass, pivots and passes to X3. X3 throws a baseball pass to X4, sprints the length of the floor and receives either a bounce or chest pass for a lay-in. X4 rebounds and throws an overhead outlet to X5. The second ball starts as the first ball is in the opposite corner. The drill is run until 20 lay-ins are made, then "Reverse" is called and it starts the other way for left handed lay-ins.

Special Value of the Drill: This is an excellent passing drill, fundamentals drill, and conditioning drill all rolled into one. It is particularly helpful in a fast breaking offense.

DAN HAYS
Northwestern Oklahoma State University

After graduation from Eastern New Mexico University, Dan Hays played in three National AAU Tournaments and against the Russian Gold Medal Olympic team. He coached for six years in high school at Roswell, New Mexico and Grants, New Mexico, taking four teams to the state tournament. He then moved to Eastern Washington University as an assistant, then to Southeastern Oklahoma State University. He is currently head basketball coach of the Northwestern Oklahoma State University Rangers.

4-ON-4 CUT THROAT: The team on offense runs a motion offense. If they score they will remain on court. A new defensive team (positioned behind the baseline) will sprint in and pick up their men, replacing the old defensive unit. The offense remains as long as they score, and they leave when they fail to do so. Any possession on a score or miss must be cleared to the coach. If the defense stops the offense, they will then

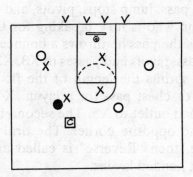

Diagram 109

go to offense as the offensive unit moves to the baseline to await their turn on defense. The offense vacates the court on a turnover. The coach can put limitations on the offense if he wishes, such as no dribbles, five passes before a shot may be taken, nothing outside 10 feet, etc. Score should be kept so that there is a "winning team."

BOB BROWN
South Portland High School, South Portland, Maine

Bob Brown graduated from Boston University in 1960. He has been a head coach at Williams High School, Rockland High School, and South Portland High School in Maine. His total 13-year record stands at 208 and 82. At South Portland High from 1974 to 1980 he has recorded 121 wins against 32 losses. In 1978 they were Western Maine Champs. In 1979 and 1980 they won the State Championship with records of 27-0 and 26-1. He was named conference "Coach of the Year" in 1978, 1979, and 1980 and he was state "Coach of the Year" in both 1979 and 1980. His present unbeaten string stands at 49.

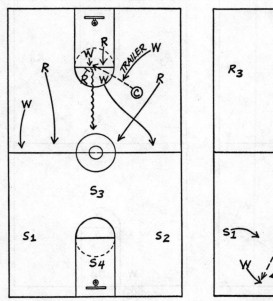

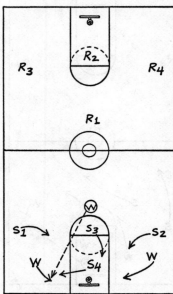

Diagram 110A   Diagram 110B

"444": If the name of your game is "fast break and pressure basketball," then "444" is a must drill. It combines transition basketball with constant pressure. It allows you to work on your pressure as well as against them. It is competitive, exciting, and extremely popular with all players.

Your squad is divided into three groups of 4 (names depend on the colors of your reversible practice jerseys). A Red team, a White team, and a Skin team. If you have more team members, then let them alternate with players on one of the groups. Each group is assigned a particular press. Red Team: 2-2-1. White Team: 1-2-1-1. Skins: Man-to-man run and jump (each skin must know his M-M responsibilities before the drill starts). The back of the Zone presses is played by the players playing defense at the other end (R1 & R2 in Diagram 110D; S1 & S2 in Diagram 110F). They cannot go over the mid-court but have

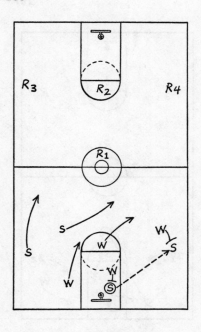

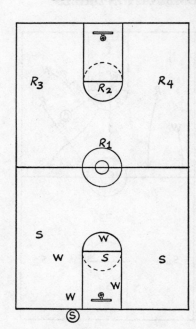

Diagram 110C   **Diagram 110D**

complete freedom in their end. The defensive men who are waiting at the foul line extended (S1 and S2 in Diagram 110D) cannot step onto the court until the ball has passed by them.

The coach starts the drill by throwing the ball (Diagram 110A) to anyone in the R&W group waiting to grab the ball and fast break. The team that doesn't grab the ball tries to stop the fast break up to the mid-court line. In this example W1 grabs the ball and starts the fast break as the other W's fill the lanes or become the trailer. S3 and S4 play defense against the fast break and S1 and S2 help on defense as soon as the ball goes by them (Diagram 110B). Both teams rebound the shot. The offensive team (W) continues to try to score on an offensive rebound. On a defensive rebound (Diagram 110C) S starts a fast break as W takes away the outlet pass or double teams the ball or uses some other tactic to try to get the ball back. R1 and R2 are ready to play defense at the other end.

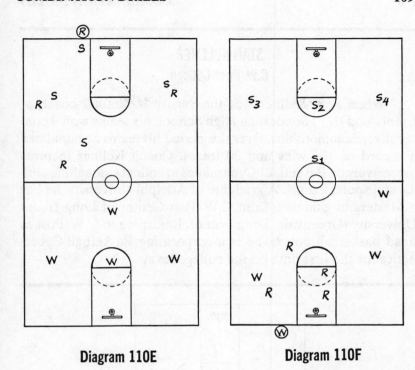

Diagram 110E   **Diagram 110F**

If a basket is scored by W (Diagram 110D) they go into their press (1-2-1-1). S attacks the press with whatever your running responsibilities against pressure are. This vital aspect of your game gets constant practice during this drill.

Diagram 110E shows what happens when the S team scores and Diagram 110F shows R scoring. The players playing defense should constantly be made to rotate so everyone works on stopping the fast break. We use this drill about three times a week. It is competitive to 7 baskets, with the losing teams running the lines. If no one reaches 7 in 10 minutes, then everyone runs.

The complete value of this drill can only be attained if your players are placed in their correct positions in your pressing game and in your running responsibilities. This will take careful planning, but it will be well worth it. It is a good idea to change players and presses each week.

STAN KELLNER
C.W. Post College

When Stan Kellner was the varsity basketball coach at Brentwood (NY) Sonderling High School, his teams won 9 consecutive championships. Over this period his teams accumulated a record of 166 wins and 30 losses. Coach Kellner lectures extensively on Basketball-Cybernetics at colleges, coaching clinics and sports camps. A graduate of Adelphi University, he has a Masters in guidance from C.W. Post Center of Long Island University (Greenvale, Long Island). Returning to C.W. Post as head basketball coach, he is incorporating Basketball-Cybernetics for the first time on the college level.

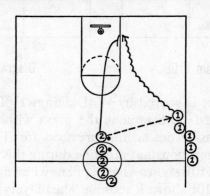

Diagram 111

"POWER" LAYUP DRILL:

1. There are two lines of players facing the basket. Each team gets the ball for one minute.

2. Two balls are used. The passer must have one foot in the center circle. The shooter must keep one foot behind "hash" mark.

3. The team with the fewest points wins. Each missed shot or fumble counts as a score.

4. #2 passes to #1; #1 drives to the basket, seals #2 on his hip and performs a jump layup, protecting the ball and shot with the body. The shooter jumps off both feet.

5. Bad passes don't count, but time is lost by the passing team.

6. #1 returns to the shooting line. #2 returns to the passing line.

7. The teams switch after one minute. Work the left side game after the right side is completed.

DAN FUKUSHIMA
Independence High School, San Jose, California

In his quarter century of coaching basketball on three levels, Dan Fukushima has compiled a total of 353 wins against 189 losses. His basketball activities have taken him to three continents. He conducted basketball clinics in Japan in 1964 and at the World University Games in 1968, and in 1973 he was advisory coach of the U.S. Prep All-Stars to Mexico under the auspices of the Cultural and Athletic Exchange Program. In 1968 he was coach of the West team in the Northern California East-West All Star Game. In 1973 he was selected as National "Coach of the Year." He has just wound up ten years as National Basketball Chairman and will complete ten years as State Basketball Chairman. He still serves as the Naismith Hall of Fame Chairman.

PRESSURE FREE THROW AND 2-ON-1 DRILL: Numbers 1 and 2 position themselves so they can rebound the missed free throw. They should also determine beforehand which will inbound the ball in the event the shot is made. The free throw shooter takes the free throw. Whether or not he makes the free throw, he must hustle back on defense quickly enough to touch the baseline with his hand and then defend against the two-on-one. If he makes the free throw, he gains precious time to come up and force the offense into mistakes. A slow or lazy player will find the offense practically climbing up his back. If he holds up the offense for five seconds, forces an error or a missed shot, he wins. Players rotate positions. If the shooter makes the free throw, he gains time because the rebounders will have to inbound the ball legitimately to start the break. It is possible to make this a 3-on-1, a 3-on-2, or a 4-on-3 drill merely by adding more stations.

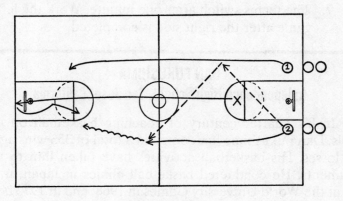

Diagram 112

Special Value of the Drill: The drill rewards players for doing things well and penalizes for mistakes. It puts pressure on free throw shooting in a practical practice situation while encouraging hustle on both offense and defense.

DICK FICHTNER
University of the Pacific

Dick Fichtner got his start in coaching as an assistant at Occidental College in Los Angeles in 1964 and compiled a 52-17 record in three years as freshman coach. After six seasons as an assistant at Occidental, he was elevated to the head coaching spot and he responded with three consecutive runner-up finishes in the Southern California Intercollegiate Athletic Conference and a 48-31 overall won-lost record. He then became the number one assistant to Stan Morrison for six seasons at the University of the Pacific. In 1979 he became the Head Basketball coach at UOP.

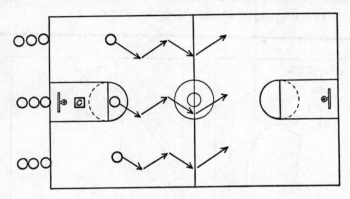

Diagram 113

RETREAT-TRANSITION DRILL: There are three players on the floor at the free throw line extended facing the coach. They retreat with vision on the ball and coach at all times. The coach dictates retreat angle of the players by moving the ball from side to side, then finally throwing or rolling the ball to any area of the gym. All three players pursue the ball and then go on a three man fast break.

Special Value of the Drill: The drill teaches players to retreat with vision, quickly react to a turnover, and make the transition to offense instantly.

DON BAILEY
Limon High School, Limon, Colorado

Don Bailey coached at Branson High School in Branson, Colorado for one year before coming to Limon High. In his six-year tenure there he has won 108 games while losing only

26 for a winning percentage of .810. Limon has lost only one home game since January 1975. Branson is the only team in Colorado that has beaten Merino (four-time state champ) in the last four years. Bailey was the coach of the South in the All-State game in 1978, and in the last four years he has had three players who played in the All-State game.

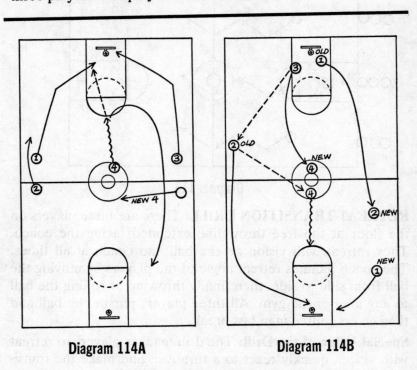

Diagram 114A   **Diagram 114B**

SORM: This is the name we have given to the drill. The letters stand for **S**hooter, **O**utlet, **R**ebounder, and **M**iddle. *Middle* — the ball starts here. He dribbles forward far enough to make a defensive man commit, then comes to a jump stop and passes to the man on his left. He then turns right and will be the shooter at the other end. *Shooter* — He comes forward at the same time as the middle man, then cuts at a 45° angle just past the free throw line to the basket. He then makes a right turn and sprints to the hash mark at the other end to become the outlet.

Rebounder — He comes forward at the same time as the middle man, then cuts at a 45° angle just past the free throw line to the basket, rebounds the ball, lands facing out, throws a baseball pass to the outlet man. He then goes to the hash mark to receive the pass from the outlet man to start the drill back the other way. *Outlet* — He starts in the back court and comes forward past the hash mark to receive the ball and land in a jump stop, pivots to the outside, passes to the middle, then sprints to the other end to become the rebounder. #1 (shooter) becomes #2 (outlet). #2 (outlet) becomes #3 (rebounder). #3 (rebounder) becomes #4 (middle). #4 (middle) becomes #1 (shooter). This drill was given to me by Harry Miller, former coach at Wichita State, and I have modified it to fit my needs.

JAMES BOEHEIM
Syracuse University

After a very successful basketball career at Syracuse, Jim Boeheim did post-graduate work, played in the Eastern League and helped with the basketball program before being named fulltime assistant in 1969. In 1976 he was named head coach, and Syracuse University's fortunes have been bright ever since. Through three campaigns he has averaged nearly 25 wins a season, won a pair of in-season tournaments (the Carrier Classic and the Lobo Classic), two ECAC titles, and taken SU to three NCAA tournaments. His 74-14 record includes two 26-4 seasons, setting a record for the most wins in a season in the school's history. In 1981 Syracuse reached the NIT finals.

3-BALL FULL COURT LAYUP DRILL: Three balls are used in this drill. They begin in the positions shown in the diagram. The ball is passed to the man at the free throw line and returned to the man driving in for the layup. After the shot a new man rebounds the ball, passes out to the man at the free throw line, receives a return pass, and drives down court as quickly as possible. Again, he passes to the man at the free throw line, receives a return pass, and drives in for a layup. The team must make 120 layups in four minutes. The inside men (passers) are rotated every minute.

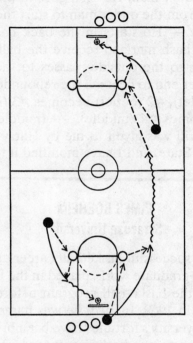

Diagram 115

Special Value of the Drill: This is the drill we use at the end of practice. It is a *team* drill. If one man makes a mistake it hurts everybody. If the team fails to make 120 layups, we go again. The drill is used in place of sprints.

BURRALL PAYE
William Fleming High School, Roanoke, Virginia

Burrall Paye has coached at three schools: Powell Valley High School (8 years), Whitttle Springs High School (8 years), and currently William Fleming High School in Roanoke, Virginia. His record now stands at 328-81. In 18 years his teams have won 12 district championships, 6 regional championships, and one state championship (finished second twice and in the top four two other times). He has had one undefeated season (28-0 and two other undeafeated regular seasons. He has won 22 different "Coach of the Year" awards. He was assistant coach twice (1973 and 1976) in the state's annual all-star game, and was head coach once (1974). He is the author of four books for Parker Publishing Company: *The Winning Power of Pressure Defense in Basketball, Secrets of the Passing-Dribbling Game Offense, Coaching the Full Court Man-to-Man Press,* and *Complete Coaching Guide to Basketball's Match-Up Zone.*

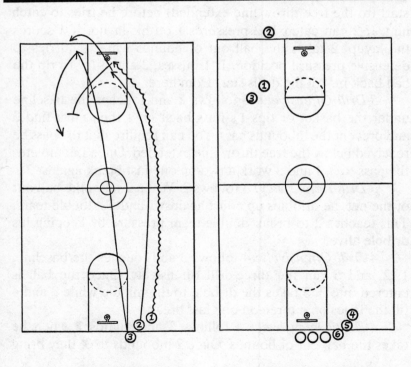

Diagram 116A   **Diagram 116B**

3-4-5-6 DRILL: This drill can be worked using from three to six players, depending on the objectives of the coach. We divide the drill into eight categories: 3-Drill Offensively, 3-Drill Defensively, 4-Drill Offensively, 4-Drill Defensively, 5-Drill Offensively, 5-Drill Defensively, 6-Drill Offensively, 6-Drill Defensively. The drills are easily remembered: for example, 5-Drill Defensively means five players involved, three of whom are defenders; 5-Drill Offensively forecasts five players, three of whom are attackers. For better defensive results, you can require that all offensive players without the ball stay behind the advancement of the ball. For better offensive results, you should turn the attackers loose with parts of your offense.

Each of the eight drills begin the same (as in Diagram 116A). 1 drives the length of the court. 2 gives 1 a 15 foot start (to the free throw line extended) before he tries to catch him. If 2 can catch 1, 2 pressures 1 on his layup. If 1 scores the layup, 2 takes the ball out of bounds while 1 hurries to defensive pressure position. If 1 misses, 2 and 3 try to tip the ball back in. All the drills start from here.

3-Drill Offensively: 3 follows 2 and touches the baseline under the basket or tips 1's miss back in. 1 then must find 3 and prevent the inbounds pass. You can require that the pass be received below the free throw line extended. Once 1 completes the pass to 3, 1 and 3 work a two-on-one fast break against 2.

3-Drill Defensively: 3 follows 2. When 2 takes the ball out of the net, he dribbles up court against 1 and 3's double team. This teaches 2 to break double-team pressure by keeping his dribble alive.

4-Drill Offensively: 4 follows 3 and touches the baseline. 1, 2, and 3 run the three-drill offensively. Once the ball is entered into 3, 3 takes the dribble to the middle while 2 and 4 fill the lanes on a three-on-one fast break.

4-Drill Defensively: 4 follows 3 and guards 2 when he takes the ball out of bounds. Once 2 inbounds to 3, they bring the ball up against 1 and 4. 1 and 4 can run and jump or use any defensive strategy you prescribe. 1 and 4 could double 3 on the inbounds pass if you prefer. 4 could shortstop or centerfield.

5-Drill Offensively: 1, 2, 3, and 4 run four-drill offensively. 5 follows 4 and prevents 2 from passing the ball in to 4. Both 5 and 1 face guard, deny, or use techniques you intend as part of your pressure defense. Once 2 enters the ball into 3 or 4, the three of them fast break against 1 and 5. At the conclusion of the three-on-two break, 1 and 5 can, if you wish, bring the ball back against the point attacker in a 2-on-1 break.

5-Drill Defensively: 1, 2, 3 and 4 run four-drill defensively. 5 follows 4 but stops near the free-throw line. He can double-team 3 to prevent the inbounds pass (shortstop). Or he can play off 3 while 1 face-guards 3, helping prevent the lob (centerfield). Or you can use other techniques you intend as part of your team pressure defense. Once the ball is inbounded, 2 and 3 attack while 1, 4 and 5 defend. 1, 4 and 5 can double-team and shoot the gap or run and jump or use any team defensive maneuver you want to employ.

6-Drill Offensively: 1, 2, 3, 4 and 5 run the five-drill offensively. 6 follows 5 and stays on the baseline until 2 hits 3 or 4. Then 2, 3, 4 and 6 fast break against 1 and 5, 6 or 2 becomes the trailer (pre-determined by you) in the fast break. This allows you to run your first and second wave of your fast break against pressure.

6-Drill Defensively: 1, 2, 3, 4 and 5 run five-drill defensively. 6 follows 5 and touches the baseline. 5 keeps pressure on 6, preventing the inbounds pass from 2 to 6. 4 can pressure 2, or 4 can drip off 2 and play centerfield or double-team one of the inbounds pass receivers (shortstop). After the ball is inbounded, 1, 4 and 5 can run and jump, double-team and shoot the gap, or any defensive measure you prefer against 2, 3 and 6. If 1, 4 and 5 steal a pass or dribble, they fast break. If 2, 3 and 6 can break the press, they fast break.

DON GOSZ
Dominican High School, Milwaukee, Wisconsin

Don Gosz is a veteran of 18 years of coaching in Wisconsin high schools, the last four having been spent at Dominican High School in Milwaukee. His last two Dominican teams won 49 games while losing only one in winning two consecutive WISAA State Championships. He is currently working on a 57 game win streak. His 1978-79 team was Number 1 in both the AP and UPI polls. Coach Gosz was named Milwaukee *Sentinel's* 1978 Coach of the Year and was selected to coach the South A large school team in the 1st annual Wisconsin High School Coaches Association All-Star Game held in Madison.

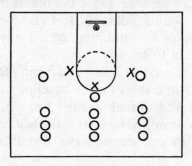

Diagram 117

3-ON-3 HALF COURT: The defense cannot let the offense score for three successive tries. The defense cannot let the offense get an offensive rebound. The defense cannot foul (if a foul occurs, the player shoots two shots. He must make both to have the series start again. If one throw is missed, it is the defense's advantage). The X's must stay on defense until they stop the O's three times in succession. The O's alternate chances with each group only going one time. The O team that is stopped by the X team is the one that goes on defense.

Special Value of the Drill: I feel the drill teaches defensive competitiveness since the players must stay on defense unless they successfully stop the offense. It also teaches offensive patience and good shot selection since players do not want to fail and be forced to play defense.

MIKE SCHULER
Rice University

Mike Schuler began his coaching career at Marietta High School where he spent two seasons. After one year at Sabina High, Bobby Knight hired him as his assistant at the U.S. Military Academy. In 1966 he returned to his alma mater to assist Jim Snyder. He spent three seasons there and then, in 1969, accepted the head coaching job at Virginia Military Institute. He left VMI in 1972 to become an aid at the University of Virginia in the strong Atlantic Coast Conference. In 1977, Schuler accepted the head coaching job at Rice University.

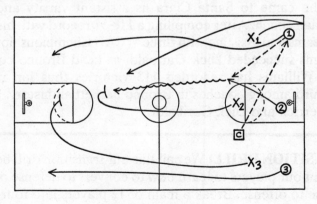

Diagram 118

3-ON-3 PRESSURE: Three offensive players line up on the end line facing the court. Three defensive players line up at the foul line or foul line extended facing the offensive players. The coach, who is somewhere inbounds, passes the ball to one of the offensive players. The defensive player opposite this offensive player must sprint to the end line and then sprint back to play defense. The other two defensive players retreat immediately to set up a defensive tandem at the opposite basket. The three offensive players attempt to advance the ball and score before the third defensive player can sprint back to help on defense.

Special Value of the Drill: The drill teaches principles involved in defensing the fast break. It instills the importance of continuous effort on defense. It provides offensive work in the 3-on-2 area of the fast break.

CARROLL WILLIAMS
University of Santa Clara

Carroll Williams began his coaching career 18 years ago at Ranier High School in Seattle, Washington. Three years later, in 1963, after a two-year stint at Blackford High School in San Jose, he came to Santa Clara as assistant varsity and head freshman coach. After compiling a 118-51 record with his freshman teams and assisting with three WCAC Championship teams, Williams succeeded Dick Garibaldi as head Bronco coach in 1970. Williams has recorded 113 victories thus far, ranking him third among coaches in Bronco basketball history, behind Bob Ferrick and Dick Garibaldi.

TRANSITION DRILL: We call this our transition drill because we want our players to learn how to convert to defense or from defense to offense. Break a team of 12 players into four teams of three. Example: X, O, A and B. O is on offense first and X is on defense first. The A team will come in next on defense and B will follow that.

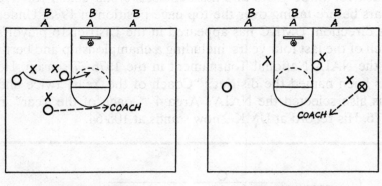

Diagram 119A   **Diagram 119B**

Objects of the Drill: The offense attempts to score and stay on the floor. If the defense takes it away, they convert to offense, and the O's are off the floor and at the end of the line. The A's step in quickly and pick up a man and attempt to take the ball away from the X's. If the O's score, the X's are off and the A's take their place. Whenever the ball goes through the basket, is stolen, or rebounded, it first must go to the coach who controls the tempo of the drill. He can give the ball immediately to the offense if the defense is not alert. You may set up a part of your offense, an opponent's offense, or just play random set. The first team to reach 5 baskets wins and the others run. It is an excellent alertness and reaction drill. It is very competitive with good, live rebounding situations.

DARRELL CORWIN
University of Missouri — Kansas City

After coaching in the North Kansas City School District for four years, Darrell Corwin joined the Health and Physical Education Department at UMKC where he is currently an assistant professor in his thirteenth year. He was head baseball coach for three years and assistant basketball coach for five years before taking over the top cage position in 1973. Under his direction, UMKC has appeared in the District 16 playoffs each of the last four years, including a championship and berth in the NAIA National Tournament in the 1976-77 season. He has been named the district's "Coach of the Year" twice and was also selected the NAIA's Area 4 "Coach of the Year" in 1976. His record at UMKC now stands at 105-64.

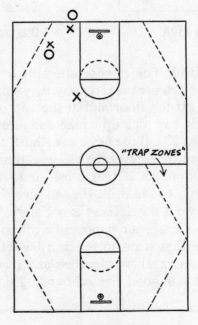

Diagram 120

2-ON-2 PLUS 1: The goal of this drill is for the two offensive players to take the ball full court and try to score. The three defensive players try to get the ball by "trapping" with two players anywhere on the court but preferably in the "trap zones," while the third player, the "anticipator," tries for the steal. After the defense steals the ball they try to score 3 on 2.

Special Value of the Drill: This is a good drill for offensive players. It teaches ball handling and passing against full court zone pressure. It is an excellent drill for defensive players. It teaches "trapping" and "anticipation" that are used a great deal in zone presses.